Dancing With Thieves

One Woman's Incredible Journey from the World of Theatre to the Streets, Slums and Prisons of São Paulo, Brazil

CALLY MAGALHÃES

Sarah
GRACE
PUBLISHING
Dyslexic Friendly

First published 2020 by Sarah Grace Publishing,
an imprint of Malcolm Down Publishing Ltd
www.malcolmdown.co.uk

24 23 22 21 20   7 6 5 4 3 2 1

British Library Cataloguing in Publication Data
A catalogue record for this book is available from the British Library.

ISBN 978-1-912863-58-7

Cover design by Esther Kotecha
Photography by Jessica Galter and Olga Gotz
Art direction by Sarah Grace

Printed in the UK

Dedication

This book is dedicated to my two sons, Benjamin and Joseph. Thank you for all you have taught me, and for all the love you constantly show me.

This book is also for all my other 'sons' and 'daughters', the ones who call me 'Mum', and whom I love as my own.

Dedication

As one person I cannot change the world, but I can change the world of one person.
Anonymous

Contents

What others are saying about
Dancing with Thieves...

Wow, this book is amazing. Cally's personality and energy dance on the pages. With an open and honest approach, she takes the reader with her on some remarkable adventures, testifying to God's faithfulness in the midst of exciting, terrifying and heart-wrenching situations, and demonstrating what relying on God is really all about. I can't wait to see what happens in the next chapters of Cally's life!

Frances Miles
Chief Relationship Officer, Stewardship

This inspirational book is a constant journey from darkness to light: equipped with a profound understanding of theatre, play and performance and a deep faith, Cally has brought hope and positive attitudes to the lost, the desperate and the unloved. Like the biblical couple on the road to Emmaus, she talks of Jesus and shocking events whilst intervening on His behalf into the lives of those who might appear to be beyond human reach.

Kenneth Pickering
Hon Professor of Drama, University of Kent and co-founder of the Institute for Arts in Therapy and Education, London

Cally Magalhães' memoir is a gripping page-turner of an autobiography. With a novelist's eye for descriptive detail, Cally invites us to accompany her on her astonishing journey from England to India and Estonia, and finally to São Paulo, Brazil. We join her as she follows a trail of signs and blessings to bring relief, hope and healing to people who need help, wherever they may be – in the streets, the *favelas*, the prisons or hidden under bridges. She describes in moving detail the transformational work of The Eagle Project, using psychodrama and Restorative Justice in Brazilian prisons. To read this book is to be inspired by the positive change one person can bring to so many individual lives – changing the world one person at a time. Cally has much to teach us about being fully present for all of life's events and challenges. With hard-won wisdom and deep reflection, she describes a life based on faith and gratitude, encapsulated in her ringing sentence, 'When you help people who have nothing, then you realise you have everything.' Her memoir has lessons for us all about what it means to walk the earth with grace and love.

Clark Baim, PhD
Director, Birmingham Institute for Psychodrama, UK
Founder of Geese Theatre Company UK

An inspirational story of heartbreak, faith, hope and joy. It is wonderful to see how God has shaped and called Cally, using some of the most challenging experiences of her life to help transform the lives of the most vulnerable. A beautiful journey of discovery and the transformational power of love, from the small town of Harpenden to the streets and prisons of São Paulo.

Nicola Temple
Head of Inspired Individuals, Tearfund

Make no mistake, this is a faith-building book. A truly biblical hero's journey in which an ordinary woman answers a seemingly crazy call from God and where God constantly shows up throughout the journey in remarkable and miraculous ways. You will be moved, amazed, challenged and inspired by the profound humanity on show in all its beauty and ugliness, and how one person has impacted a nation with God's supernatural help. A timeless story of hope amidst the darkness.

Tim Richardson
Director, Waverley Learning

Cally's amazing story, so vividly told in *Dancing with Thieves*, will draw you into every stage of her personal journey of faith and inspire you to believe... Believe that God is present everywhere, from the suffering, pain, raw joy and community of the *favelas* of São Paulo, to the seemingly 'perfect' suburbs of London. Believe that God still is in the business of making *all things new*,[1] with no life or circumstance too far gone for Him to restore and use for his purposes in the world. Believe that our human failings and failures, when brought before God, bring us to the place of revelation, hope and new beginnings. Believe that what is impossible for the experts of this world, is totally possible for the creator and sustainer of all things. I had the privilege of coaching Cally during a part of her incredible journey and my life was inspired as a witness to her faithful, tenacious and dedicated response to God's call on her life. What a gift now for many more seekers, sojourners and followers to be inspired as well through this wonderful memoir.

Thomas G. Yaccino
Global Connector-Coach-Consultant

---

[1] Revelation 21:5, NKJV.

Foreword

It was a hot, sunny afternoon in São Paulo as the Consulate's Land Rover made its way slowly through the city's heavy traffic. My wife, Dilsa, and I felt a mix of apprehension and curiosity at what lay ahead.

I was serving as the British Consul General in São Paulo and, although my main role was to promote British trade with Brazil, I was always keen to support British citizens who were involved in social projects. So, we had been pleased to accept Cally's invitation to visit the young offenders' institution in São Paulo where she was leading psychodrama therapy workshops as part of 'The Eagle Project'.

Cally was waiting for us at the visitors' entrance and helped us through the tight security arrangements. She explained to us that through psychodrama, the young offenders acted out the roles of other people who had been involved with their crime. By taking on the role of the victim, for example, they understood what it felt like to be robbed at gunpoint on the city's streets; or, assuming the role of a close family member, what it felt like for their family to see them locked up for their crime.

Meeting the young offenders themselves and the staff showed me very clearly the high regard in which The Eagle Project was held. For the young men, it offered hope for a new start away from crime. 'We're seeing amazing results,' Cally told us, 'and most of the boys who have joined our workshops have not reoffended.'

Before heading back to the Consulate, we talked some more with Cally about her own background. She told us that she had trained in drama as a student back in the UK, but had felt called to come to Brazil and to work with the poorest of the poor in the city's sprawling *favelas* or shanty towns. That work had taken her to the prisons and here she was, with her young family, leading a life of dedicated ministry among the downtrodden of Brazil's largest city and making wonderful use of her drama training in the prisons of São Paulo.

In the days after the visit, Dilsa and I reflected on the many questions that we would like to ask Cally. How did she become a Christian? How did she know that she was being called to Brazil? How did she survive financially?

Here, in this book, are the answers to the many questions we wanted to ask about Cally's life. It is a beautifully written story, absolutely compelling from the start to the end. She tells of her early life and family circumstances, her initial success in training to be a professional dancer, her setbacks, her joys and her triumphs, the support and encouragement from many people she met along the way, and her pride and delight in her two young sons.

It was out of initial setbacks that her Christian faith was born and with that came a burning sense of social justice. Horrified at the sight of the thousands of homeless people, including many young infants, trying to sleep on the railway stations of Mumbai, she vowed to devote her life to one of service to these most vulnerable people in whatever part of the world she was called to serve. As her faith was nourished and strengthened, she found the courage to follow her calling and a confidence that there was no obstacle, whether practical, financial or emotional, that could not be overcome with God's help.

I hope that you enjoy reading Cally's story as much as I did. It is a remarkable account of a life devoted to Christian service among people, and in a country, that she loves unconditionally.

John Doddrell
Her Majesty's Consul General in São Paulo, 2010-14

Introduction

When I was seventeen years old, I danced for Queen Elizabeth II, at the Royal Albert Hall in London. It was, without doubt, one of the most wonderful experiences of my life. My dream was to be a professional dancer, and I dedicated my childhood and teenage years to pursue my goal. My dream, however, was not to be, and my life took a very different route.

This book, *Dancing with Thieves*, is the story of my life so far, and of my work as a missionary during the last twenty-one years in São Paulo, Brazil. Almost all names have been changed, and there are many details of certain relationships and situations that I can't describe, to protect people's integrity. However, I've attempted to tell the rest as faithfully as possible. This is a story of broken dreams, and of my heart broken more times than I could ever have imagined.

Most of all, it's a story of faith and love. Finding the faith to serve God in short-term missions in India and Estonia, and then long-term in Brazil. My work has taken me to the streets, the slums and the prisons, and there I've learned what God's love is all about. He has taught me to love the unloved and the rejected, those who have been discarded by society, showing them His love and hope for a new future.

If you're a Christian I pray this book will encourage you in your faith. Maybe my story will help you find your 'calling' in God, if you haven't already. I pray it will encourage you to seek God, and hear His voice. I pray it will teach you to step out in faith, to be brave and know that He's with you, wherever you go.

If you're not a Christian then I hope this book will draw you nearer to God. I pray you'll be encouraged and challenged by the stories and miracles God has done, and want to know this miracle-working God for your self.

Maybe you're struggling, in your faith, in your work, with your family, or whatever difficult situations you are facing. I pray this book will encourage you to persevere. I pray you will discover just how much God loves you, and know that He cares about even the smallest details of your life.

I never imagined I would write a book, but here it is! I pray you will be blessed.

Chapter One: The First Day

Take the first step in faith.
You don't have to see the whole staircase, just take the first step.
(Attributed to Martin Luther King Jr)[2]

Life is cheap in Brazil. Tens of thousands of adults, teenagers and children are murdered every year. I became aware of this sad truth on my first visit to São Paulo in 1998.

I arrived at the airport and was taken straight to the *favela* (the Portuguese name for slum). I had been told this would be my home for the next month, but I soon discovered the plans had changed. The director of the project greeted me, Brazilian-style, with a warm, friendly hug.

'Welcome, Cally,' she said. 'We're so glad you've arrived. However, I'm so sorry to tell you, but you can't stay here after all. Something terrible happened here last night. It's just too dangerous.'

Maribel had a kind face, and a gentle voice. Her eyes were red, and it was obvious that she'd been crying. I could tell she was shaken and upset, and I didn't know what to say.

---

[2] Manning Marable, Leith Mulling (eds), *Let Nobody Turn Us Around* (Lanham, MD: Rowman & Littlefield Publishers, 1999).

I looked around me. Everything seemed 'normal'. There was a low building on one side of the courtyard with classrooms and a kitchen. The church building was on the other side, and a large space in-between where about fifty children were playing.

Two boys raced past me, nearly knocking me over in their haste. Their eyes were fixed on the battered old kite they were desperately trying to keep in the air. One held the string, and the other ran behind, laughing and trying to grab the kite for himself. The kite dipped, and then soared again just as they passed by me, the boys shrieking with delight.

A group of children of all ages kicked an old, half-inflated football around the courtyard. The game seemed highly competitive as they scampered barefoot in the dust and dirt. Teenage girls in skimpy shorts and low-cut T-shirts huddled in groups. They giggled at the teenage boys playing dominoes at an old wooden table nearby.

I wondered what could have happened the night before. Something so terrible it wasn't safe to stay there anymore? The sun was hot in the bright blue sky, and my arms and neck were beginning to burn.

I inhaled slowly, and the smell of freshly baked bread wafted across the courtyard from the project kitchen. At the same time, I felt quite sick from the stench of rotting rubbish outside the courtyard wall. Sweat dripped down my face, and my mouth was dry with thirst.

I looked at Diana, the young Brazilian woman who had picked me up at the airport. She was crying, and wiping her eyes with a hanky. I felt desperate to know what had happened, and then she explained.

'Just behind that wall,' she whispered, pointing to the wall behind me that divided the *favela* from the project courtyard, 'five teenagers were murdered last night. They owed money to the drug traffickers, and when they couldn't pay, they killed them.'

I stood there in shock, not knowing what to do or say.

Teenagers? I thought to myself. *Murdered? If this were the UK it would be all over the news. There would be police and reporters here investigating the case. This kind of stuff only happens in films, doesn't it?*

I looked at Diana and Maribel as they held each other tight. They were grieving the loss of five of their 'children'. I didn't know these young people, but I felt sad and shocked.

'Those teenagers had been part of our project for quite a while,' Maribel explained. 'We'd grown to love them as our own. But their home situations are so complicated, and they got involved with the wrong people. We tried to warn them, but now it's too late.'

'How much money did they owe?' I asked.

'Probably just a few reais,'[3] she answered. 'The traffickers are ruthless. If you owe money and you can't pay, then you pay with your life. It doesn't matter if you're a child or a teenager, a mum or a dad. If you owe money, you die.'

Life is definitely cheap in Brazil, I thought to myself. *Young people being murdered for just a few reais?*

This was my first day in São Paulo. I had signed up to spend a month volunteering at this project. It was run by a Brazilian organisation, in partnership with a mission organisation based in London.

Thoughts raced through my mind like a bullet train.

Would I, Cally, a thirty-four-year-old actress and drama teacher, ever be able to make a difference in this place? Would God want to use me? Would I be able to do anything to help?

I felt like I was at the base camp of Everest, with a huge climb ahead of me. I wondered what adventures God had in store for me. My mind drifted back to the conversation with my mother a few years earlier in 1994.

---

[3] Brazilian currency – the real, reais being plural.

'Mum, I need to tell you something. I think I might end up going to Brazil in the future. I sense God's calling me to work there.'

My mother had raised her head from the newspaper she was reading. She looked at me over the rim of her reading glasses, and said simply, 'You are forbidden to go!'

My dad had said nothing, and then muttered, 'That doesn't sound like a good idea, Cally. It's too dangerous.'

From their few words, and the expressions on their faces, I sensed their concern. It was obvious my mother couldn't forbid me to go as I was already a grown adult. I could have replied with several reasons to justify myself, but decided to keep quiet. My dad was giving me 'the look' that meant, 'don't start an argument'. I had no fixed plans about Brazil at that moment, so it wasn't worth making a fuss. I changed the subject, and we moved on to talking about roses and weather, and nice things like that.

Now it was September 1998 and I'd managed to convince my mother that this was just a short trip. A few weeks before I left for Brazil, I visited my parents' house, and broached the subject again.

'Mum, you remember a few years ago I mentioned about going to Brazil? Well, I've finally decided to visit.' She looked at me with one eyebrow raised. 'Don't worry, Mum, it's just for a month,' I said, throwing my arms around her and hugging her tight.

'Well, if it's just one month, I'm sure that will be alright,' she replied. 'As long as you're safe, that's all that matters.'

'Of course I'll be safe, Mum. God always keeps me safe.'

'I still think it's too dangerous, Cally,' my dad muttered, shifting in his seat.

'Honestly, Dad, if God's sending me then I'll be fine. I really believe He'll protect me.'

My parents didn't have any experience of missions or being 'called' by God, and it was difficult for them to understand. I have to admit I did feel vindicated a couple of weeks after this conversation. I was in my house in Milton Keynes, England, on a quiet Sunday afternoon. I was sitting comfortably on my sofa watching television, and enjoying a box of Maltesers, my favourite chocolates with a crisp honeycomb centre.

I threw the first one into my mouth, chewing and swallowing it with delight. Then I threw the next. It became stuck on the roof of my mouth, so I gently pried it off with my tongue. The rest of the box I allowed to dissolve slowly in my mouth, savouring the chocolate coating of each one as it melted into the honeycomb.

There was a football match on the television and I was cheering for Brazil. Without warning I heard a loud 'BANG' from the direction of my kitchen.

What on earth was that? I thought to myself, and with my heart racing, ran to see what had happened. Imagine my surprise when I saw a bullet hole in the middle of my kitchen window! I stood there, in shock, for a few seconds. There were no sounds of gunshots or shouting.

Then I heard the sound of footsteps racing down the alley beside my house. I ran to the front door but by the time I reached the alley it was empty. I rushed into the house, and picked up the phone. I dialled my parent's number, and my father answered.

'Dad, Dad, is that you? You're never going to guess what just happened. A few minutes ago, someone shot at my kitchen window. I think it must have been an airgun. There's a bullet hole in my kitchen window. See, Dad. It isn't just Brazil that's dangerous. I could get shot just living here in Milton Keynes!'

Standing in the *favela* a few weeks later I realised things were a little more dangerous than I had thought. I imagined my return to England, coming down the steps of the plane, in a coffin! And my mum saying, 'I told you so,' to my dad.

A few hours earlier I had arrived in Guarulhos International Airport, São Paulo. It had been a busy few days, saying goodbye to friends and setting off alone, into the unknown. I had hardly slept on the plane, imagining where I would be staying and the people I would meet. I grabbed my suitcase at the baggage reclaim and walked purposefully into the arrivals hall.

This was my first trip to Brazil to 'test the waters' for a possible long-term commitment. I was so excited to be putting my feet on Brazilian soil, at last. Taxi drivers with special white caps tried to offer me their services. I had no idea what they were saying, but waved my hands trying to demonstrate that I didn't need a taxi. Diana, the Brazilian coordinator of the project I was to be working with, had agreed to pick me up at the airport.

I scoured the faces of the relatives and friends waiting at the arrivals' gate. I looked at each person expectantly, hoping to find Diana. No one seemed to recognise me. The atmosphere was one of joy and excitement as passengers arrived, and friends and relatives greeted them with hugs and kisses. I instantly felt at home in this welcoming land, despite my lone arrival, with no hugs yet.

I looked at all the signs being held up, hoping to see my name on one of them. After a few minutes I reached the unfortunate conclusion that no one had come to meet me. I didn't have a mobile phone, or any number to contact Diana.

Now what am I going to do? I thought. I decided to find the information desk, and asked them to announce my arrival over the loudspeaker. I waited expectantly, hoping Diana had heard the announcement. That didn't work either. I slumped down in a chair near the door of the arrivals' hall, and tried to convince myself that she would soon be there to collect me.

I knew very little about the Brazilian culture at that time, especially not about time-keeping. Now, after years of living in São Paulo, I have learned simply to wait. Almost always the person is delayed in traffic, and will arrive sooner or later. However, without the knowledge I have now, I began to feel decidedly concerned.

What if she never comes to pick me up? I have no idea where to go, or where I am supposed to be staying. What if I have to get on the next plane back home?

Questions and paranoid thoughts raced through my mind, and tears pricked the back of my eyes. I desperately tried to hold myself together, as crying would look so pathetic and weak. I was a grown woman after all, thirty-four years old, and an experienced traveller. I felt tears welling up in my eyes, and struggled to deal with my potential abandonment.

After about half an hour of anguish, she arrived. A young, energetic Brazilian woman, she suddenly appeared out of nowhere, gave me my long-awaited hug, and whisked me out of the airport. She apologised for being late, and I decided not to mention my thirty minutes of agony.

I was exhausted. I scolded myself for not sleeping on the flight, and for all the unnecessary emotional energy I'd used up at the airport. I don't remember much about the journey, but a few details remain in my mind. The traffic was crazy, everyone driving as close as possible to the car in front. The motorbike riders raced along the motorway at high speed, beeping their horns and weaving in and out of the car lanes.

We slowed to a stop in the rush-hour traffic, and I saw people selling snacks and bottles of water, walking between the lanes of traffic, offering their wares.

'Diana, does this happen everywhere, people selling like this?' I asked.

'Yes,' she replied, 'especially when there are traffic jams in the rush hour. Many poor people work like this to earn money. Even on the motorways the traffic's often very slow or stationary.'

'Isn't it dangerous?' I asked.

'Yes, very,' she replied, 'especially as they need to avoid the motorbikes travelling at high speed between the cars.'

I also remember seeing tiny little houses made out of brick, and built all higgledy-piggledy on top of each other. I had read about the *favelas* in São Paulo, and asked her about the tiny houses at the side of the road.

'Are they the *favelas*?' I asked.

'Oh no,' she replied. 'That is just poor housing.'

Just poor housing, I thought. *Then what in heaven's name are the* favelas *like?*

Chapter Two: The Dream Begins

Great dancers are not great because of their technique,
they are great because of their passion.
Martha Graham[4]

I perched on the edge of my chair, craning my neck to see the stage. The Royal Ballet Company was about to perform *Swan Lake* at the Royal Opera House, London, and I was five years old.

'We will be sitting in "the gods",' my mother had informed me a few weeks earlier. 'That means our seats will be up really high.'

I didn't fully understand what that meant at the time, but now I understood. We were sitting almost at the back of the auditorium, and we were certainly up extremely high. I felt like I was in a place very close to God or 'the gods', and definitely in some kind of heaven.

I gazed around me in wonder, admiring the deep crimson curtains and soft velvet seats. There were ladies all around me who looked like princesses, in twinkling dresses and sparkling jewellery.

Suddenly the music began, and the curtains opened to a dark, empty space. I placed the tiny theatre binoculars up to my eyes and

---

[4] American choreographer and dancer (1894-1991), http://www.quotationspage.com/quote/23843.html (accessed 19.2.20).

watched the ballerinas float onto the stage. I was enchanted to see their sleek black hair, fluffy white tutus, and their pointe shoes tied to perfection. Row after row of swans glided effortlessly from one side of the stage to the other, transporting me into another level of heaven.

Without warning the music changed and a cloud of white tutu broke through a wall of dry ice. Prima Ballerina Margot Fonteyn took centre stage, and I was entranced. I held my breath as she floated from one step to the next, her partner lifting her high above his head. She landed like a feather, her feet so delicate, and her arms so graceful.

In an instant it was all over. It seemed to have been only five minutes, and suddenly it was the interval. The curtains fell, and I turned to my mother.

'Mummy, I need to have black hair,' I declared, almost in tears. 'All the ballerinas have black hair.'

Nothing my mother could say would persuade me that some of the ballerinas were wearing wigs. There was nothing for it, my blonde hair had to go. That day marked a turning point in my short life. I decided I would become a professional dancer.

I was born in 1964, in Harpenden, Hertfordshire, and had two elder brothers. My mother had an accident while pregnant with her first child, a girl, and the baby was stillborn shortly after. She rarely talked about it, but I was definitely the long-awaited daughter after the sad loss of this first child.

My childhood memories are a mixture of happy and sad. I remember we seemed like a normal, happy, middle-class family, but behind closed doors things were very different. My parents argued almost constantly and finally separated in their old age. At the same time my mother was diagnosed with paranoid schizophrenia. Finally

I began to understand some of the crazy things that had happened in our childhood, which wouldn't be appropriate to mention here.

When I was small, there was much more stigma about seeing psychologists than there is today. My mother thought going to a psychologist would mean she had mental health problems, and she didn't want that. Life would have been very different for her, my father, my brothers and me if she had received the help she needed.

Years later I discovered that she was evacuated during the Second World War, and lost contact with her family for about eight years. I don't know if that caused trauma in her life that triggered the paranoia. After reuniting with her family, her parents and seven siblings, she left home at the age of twenty-one and never contacted them again.

My brothers and I had the immense pleasure of meeting nineteen of her long-lost relatives in 2019, for the first time. My nephew found them through the results of a DNA test, and today we have a reunited family of first and second cousins and wider family that gives us great joy.

My brothers and I were pupils at a senior school in Harpenden. Every day after school my mother drove me to dance lessons. I was eleven, and at this young age was already preparing for my future career. Looking back, I realise my parents made a huge sacrifice for me, and were so supportive of my dream to be a dancer. Every evening I did lessons in ballet, Greek dance, national, modern and tap. I prepared relentlessly for exams and festivals, performing solos, duets, trios and groups. There were medals and trophies, blisters and bruises.

Every night I did most of my homework in the car on the way home. My father developed the skill of changing gear without jolting the car even the slightest, so my handwriting was always neat and legible.

When I was thirteen there was a skiing trip advertised at school. 'Mum, Dad, can I go on the skiing trip?' I asked. 'It's in the Christmas holidays. Please let me, I've always wanted to go skiing.'

'Ski trip!' My mother exclaimed. 'I don't think so, Carolyn. If you break your leg then your dancing career is over.'

'Can I risk it?' I asked hopefully. 'I'm sure I won't break my leg.'

'I wouldn't if I were you,' my dad said gently. 'You never know what might happen. Skiing's really too dangerous for dancers.'

They're probably right, I thought to myself. *It isn't worth the risk.* So, no skiing trip. No radical sports. No serious boyfriends. My dream was to be a dancer, and nothing was going to stop me. I dreamed of performing in West End musicals, my name in lights, my dream fulfilled.

Aged fifteen I applied to the Bush Davies School of Theatre and Dance, and was called for an audition. The big day arrived, and my father drove me to East Grinstead in Sussex. My mother sat in the front seat, and I sat in the back. My stomach felt like a butterfly farm, and despite my mother's attempts to encourage me, I couldn't eat a thing. I was so desperate for this. I'd trained hard for ten long years, and this day would decide my future.

We arrived at the school, and I was told to go and change into my dance clothes. The changing room was full of excited girls, all hurriedly getting dressed, and twisting their hair into tightly knotted buns. We filed into the ballet studio, the walls adorned with huge mirrors, with various staff members seated at a long table.

Pushing myself to my limit, I performed each of the exercises at the barre, and then in the centre of the room. The other girls were all so beautiful and supple, and I wondered if I stood a chance of being accepted. We returned to the changing room, and waited to be called for the physical examination. Training at Bush Davies would be rigorous and tough, and our bodies needed to be ready for the challenge.

'Bend over slowly, Carolyn, and touch your toes, please,' the ballet teacher instructed. That was simple, and I bent down easily, and placed my hands flat on the floor.

'Stay there for a moment, please,' she said, and I felt her finger tracing a line up my back. A moment passed by, and she did the same thing again. 'Alright, you can stand up straight now,' she said. I rolled up slowly, and my eyes met hers.

'Did you know you have a curvature in your spine, Carolyn?'

'No,' I replied.

'You have a slight curve on your right side. We'll have to keep an eye on it. If you're accepted, of course.'

Slight curve, I thought, *surely that can't be too serious. Nothing's going to stop me reaching my dream.*

I put my thoughts aside, and went to sit with my mother and father. They were waiting in the reception area with the other candidates and their parents.

Most of the girls were dismissed during the afternoon. They left with their heads hung low, sobbing and inconsolable, as one after another they were told 'no'. The atmosphere was tense as the last four girls, me and three others, were called to wait outside the principal's office.

It felt like we were waiting for hours, and then I heard my name. My heart began to beat so fast I was sure I was about to have a heart attack. My throat was dry and my legs were like jelly. I walked into the principal's office with my parents. Photographs of former students decorated the walls, and I gazed at the pictures of famous ballerinas, and stars of the London West End. I stared longingly at each photo, dreaming of one day making it onto those walls. The ballet principal was speaking, and I came back down to earth with a jolt.

'Carolyn, we are delighted to offer you a place to train here with us, starting this September. You will need to work very hard, especially at your ballet technique. But we believe you have what it takes to be a professional dancer.'

One of the directors of the school added, 'She may not have perfect technique, but she'll never be out of a job.'

I heard the words I had waited so long to hear. My dream had come true.

'Thank you, thank you, oh, thank you so much,' I blurted out, and burst into tears. Everyone in the room, including my parents, laughed at my display of emotion.

'We're very happy for you, Carolyn. Congratulations, and we will see you in September.'

We left the room and I hugged my parents, crying so much I could hardly breathe. This was the best moment of my life. At last my dream would be fulfilled. I could never have imagined what the next three years would have in store for me.

A few months later and it was September 1980, and my first day at Bush Davies School. We stuffed my trunk into the back of the car and set off for East Grinstead. I sat in the back seat, imagining the dance classes, auditions and West End Musicals. I couldn't wait for the journey to be over, and gladly leapt out of the car when we arrived. We were ushered into the main hall, and were greeted by various members of staff, and the head girl.

The ballet principal greeted me first.

'Good afternoon, dear, and what is your name?'

'Good afternoon. I am Carolyn Cornes,' I replied nervously.

'Cornes!' she exclaimed loudly. 'Oh dear, that isn't a very good name for a dancer, is it? If you're going on the stage, we'll have to think of something better than that! You'll need a proper stage name.'

I felt myself blushing, and laughed politely, too embarrassed to know what to say. I had always hated my surname. My nickname at school was 'Verruca' and I was just as keen as the principal was to find a stage name as soon as possible.

The next three years were tough. I worked harder than ever, so determined to make it as a professional dancer. I have many wonderful memories of my time at Bush Davies, especially the day when we all heard some amazing news. We were just finishing our ballet class when Sue Passmore, the artistic director, called us for an important meeting. We all filed into one of the dance studios and sat in rows on the floor, wondering what was going to be announced.

Sue Passmore was standing at the front of the studio with a huge smile on her face.

'I have some wonderful news for you all,' she said. 'Bush Davies School has been invited to dance for the Queen of England, at the Albert Hall!'

There was a moment of silence, and then uproar as everyone jumped up, dancing and shouting with joy.

'The Queen?' I said to my friend next to me. 'We're going to dance for the Queen?' I could hardly believe it.

'Sit down and listen please,' Sue Passmore continued. 'We have a lot of hard work ahead of us to be ready in time for the performance. I'm sure I can count on you all to do your very best. After the performance you will line the staircase in the foyer of the Albert Hall. The Queen will walk past you as she goes down the staircase to leave the theatre. Thank you, girls, you may leave.'

We all gave a big round of applause and left the studio, chatting excitedly. The next day the rehearsal schedule was posted on the studio wall. We all gathered round to see who would be performing. A few weeks earlier we had presented a version of *Alice in Wonderland* at the Adeline Genée Theatre in East Grinstead, and excerpts from the show would be presented at the Albert Hall.

I searched for my name on the list and then found it: 'Carolyn Cornes – March Hare'.

I was ecstatic. I had been chosen to play the role of 'the March Hare' at the Albert Hall. It was a jazz trio with 'the Dormouse' and 'the Mad Hatter' and I felt so privileged to be one of the main parts in the presentation for the Queen.

The big day arrived, and we were all taken to London by coach. The atmosphere was one of excitement and exhilaration. Our parents had been invited to watch, and everyone took their seats in the theatre.

The performance began, and I burst onto the stage in the role of the March Hare. The dance was lively and fun, and I was enjoying myself so much. Then, I had to leave the stage and return on the other side of the theatre. The dress rehearsal had gone smoothly, and I knew the route to reach the other side in time for my entrance.

I ran swiftly through the corridors behind the stage, my heart beating excitedly at this wonderful experience. I hadn't seen the Queen yet, as the stage lights were too bright to see into the audience. However, I knew we would see her after the performance, and I was imagining how wonderful that would be.

To my dismay, I suddenly stopped running, realising I was lost. I should have arrived in the wings on the other side by now, but a closed door was in front of me. I had taken a wrong turn. I could hear the music playing, and it was getting closer and closer to my entrance.

Don't panic, don't panic, I said to myself, and ran back, retracing my steps. The music continued, and my heart began to beat faster and faster as I ran wildly to the other side of the stage.

Suddenly, I recognised where I was. The music changed, and just in time I burst through the wings and onto the stage. I performed with all my might, forgetting the last few moments, as the adrenaline pumped around my body. The performance ended, and the audience clapped and cheered as we took our bows. I breathed a huge sigh of relief, and rushed to change out of my costume to meet the Queen.

We all dressed quickly into our official Bush Davies dance uniform; maroon leotards, pink ballet tights, pink ballet shoes, and matching maroon velvet ribbons tied around the buns in our hair. We ran to the foyer, and positioned ourselves on the huge stairway, one dancer on each stair.

The foyer was full of people, and they all stared in awe as the Queen appeared at the top of the staircase. She looked so beautiful in her gala dress, the sequins twinkling, and the jewels shining in her crown. I could hardly breathe, I was so excited. She walked slowly down the staircase, smiling at each one of us. As she passed by me, I bowed my head and did a little curtsy as we had been instructed. When I lifted my head, she had already descended the staircase, and it was all over.

We returned to the school; I chatted excitedly to my friends all the way to East Grinstead. I couldn't believe I had just danced for the Queen of England. What an amazing experience and privilege, and she was so close to me I could have touched her!

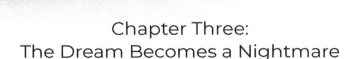

Chapter Three:
The Dream Becomes a Nightmare

The dance may have ended, but the drama is just beginning.
Cally Magalhães

'Do you do anything else except dance?' the doctor asked.

I laughed nervously and replied, 'No, not really. I just do a bit of drama, and I can sing.'

'Well, my advice is that you do that, then. Never dance again.'

The doctor had just looked at the X-rays and examined the curve in my spine. He was an orthopaedic specialist for dancers in Harley Street, London.

'For a normal person walking around, you would be fine,' he explained. 'The problem is that you are putting too much stress on your body. You can't continue like this. Your back just won't take the strain. You could even end up in a wheelchair.'

His words floated in and out of my ears as if I was dreaming.

Surely he must be wrong? I thought to myself. *After all these years of training so hard, can he really be serious that I have to stop dancing? After making it into one of the best dance schools in the country?*

I walked out of his consulting room in a daze, and closed the door. I stumbled along the pavement, thoughts running through my mind. The last few months had been really difficult. My back was so painful and each day it seemed to be getting worse.

What an idiot! He doesn't know what he's talking about. Of course I'm going to be a dancer. I can put up with the pain. I'm sure I can find a way to get better. I have to keep going. I have to achieve my dream.

I tucked my thoughts away in the back of my mind, and continued with my mission for that day. I was on my way to hire a flute at a large music shop, to begin lessons the following term.

I found my way across London and arrived at the shop. It was a music lovers' paradise, full of instruments, music books and accessories. The sound of children trying out drums, guitars and violins accosted my eardrums, as I made my way to the enquiry desk.

Without warning something strange began to happen. It seemed as though the ceiling of the shop had fallen on my head, but when I looked up, the ceiling was intact. I felt an excruciating pain across the top of my head and my forehead and face began to burn. My neck started to swell up, and I gasped for breath. I reached the counter and hurriedly asked if I could hire a flute. The shop assistant was kind and helpful and, totally unaware of my plight, she helped me fill in the forms.

About half an hour later, flute in hand, I stumbled out of the shop. Slowly and painfully I travelled back to East Grinstead on the train. I arrived at the house where I was staying, and practically fell through the front door.

'What happened to you?' Pam asked, helping me sit down on the sofa. Pam Saunders was my drama teacher from Bush Davies, and I was staying at her house during the holidays. She had asked me to take part in a one-act play that would be presented at the local drama festival, and I had accepted. I was also part of a group of students from the school who were rehearsing the show *Cabaret*. I always auditioned for the shows, and preferred staying in East Grinstead during the holidays. It was much better than going home to referee the fights between my parents.

'You look dreadful, Cally. Whatever is wrong with you?' Pam asked worriedly.

'I don't know,' I replied. 'I feel awful.'

'What happened with the doctor? What did he say?' she asked.

'Oh, some stupid stuff about me not dancing anymore.'

My throat hurt so much I could hardly speak, and my neck and head were so painful I just wanted to lie down. Pam gave me a painkiller and I made my way to bed. I tossed and turned, my forehead wet with sweat and my body hot like a furnace.

I woke up the next morning and my whole body ached. My neck was swollen and sore, but I made my way to the rehearsal. I knew I had to be there as I had learned 'the show must go on' however ill you feel. I had to rehearse my part, and I couldn't let everyone down.

'Cally, oh my goodness, what happened to you? You must have mumps!' Sue Passmore exclaimed. She was like a mum to me, and was obviously very concerned.

'I don't know, Miss Passmore,' I replied sadly. 'I don't feel well, but I can do the rehearsal.'

'I can see you're not well,' she replied. 'Your neck is so swollen. I'll phone your parents and ask them to come and pick you up. You need to go home right now, and go to the doctor.'

'No, Miss Passmore. Please don't make me go home. I want to do the show. I'll be fine in a couple of days. Please let me stay.' I begged and pleaded but she insisted I had to go home, and a few hours later my parents arrived.

'I think you have a bacterial gland infection,' my doctor stated. 'I will arrange for you to do some blood tests and the results will be ready tomorrow. Take these antibiotics and painkillers. They are very strong and should help you feel better.'

That night was worse than ever as I struggled to sleep, my throat covered with pus-filled spots. I must have fallen asleep eventually as the next morning I woke up in a pool of sweat, covered in a rash all over my body.

'Mum!' I tried to call out. 'Mum, come and see!' I called as loud as I could, but my voice was so weak and my throat so painful. Eventually she came to my bedroom to wake me up.

When she saw my face she gasped and exclaimed, 'It must be measles! I knew it from the start. I was sure that was what was wrong with you. Let's go to the doctor, he should have the blood test results by now.'

I arrived at the doctor's surgery, hardly able to walk, and slumped into a chair. A few moments later the receptionist came into the waiting room.

'I do apologise,' she said, 'but would you mind waiting in the corridor outside? You might be contagious, and I don't want to alarm the other patients.' She took a chair out of the waiting room, and I sat in the corridor.

'I am so sorry,' my doctor apologised. 'I gave you antibiotics and that was the worst thing I could have done. I have your blood test results here, and you have glandular fever! The antibiotics made it worse, and that is what caused the rash. Stop taking them, and the rash should clear up in a few days.'

'How long will this last?' I asked, hoping he would say a week or two.

'It could take weeks or maybe months. Your blood test shows a very high level of the infection. There is nothing you can do, except rest.'

I panicked, trying to find the words to reply. 'It's just that, um, I'm performing in a show at dancing school, and... um, I need to get back for rehearsals. Is that possible?' I asked hopefully. 'Oh, and I'm performing in a one-act play soon. Please may I do it?'

'No, I'm sorry,' my doctor replied firmly. 'Definitely not the show, and you can forget the play too. You won't be going anywhere for a good few weeks.'

'Oh, please let me,' I begged, holding back the tears, a lump beginning to form in my already painful throat.

'No, you're too ill,' he replied even more firmly. 'If you go against my wishes I will not be held responsible for the consequences.' He looked at my mother, and she nodded in agreement.

'Oh, and by the way, whom have you been kissing?' he asked with a cheeky grin.

Did he have to say that in front of my mother? I remembered what people said about glandular fever. They call it 'the kissing disease'. I wasn't in a serious relationship, but I had been going out with a lad from Pam Saunders' drama group. He was in the one-act play too.

I hope he hasn't got it too, I thought, and smiled a weak smile at the doctor.

I returned home feeling very dejected, and went back to my bed. The next week was a nightmare of high temperatures, pain and a sore throat. My head ached, and I felt too weak to even walk.

It was too late to take part in the show, but I was determined to do the one-act play.

'Mum, Dad, please let me do it,' I pleaded. 'There are only four of us in it, and I don't have an understudy. We've been rehearsing for weeks. It's just a one-act play so it's not very long, and I'm sure I can do it. I can't let Mrs Saunders down.'

My parents gave in to my persuasion, and drove me to East Grinstead. I laid on the back seat of the car, feeling like a zombie. My voice sounded like a strangled cat, and my throat felt like sandpaper. We arrived at the venue, and I didn't tell my parents but I felt as if I was going to faint.

'Cally, you look awful, are you sure you can do this?' Pam asked, a look of concern on her face.

'I'll be fine,' I assured her, applying my make-up with a shaky hand, and then dressing in my costume. I heard our play announced and, summoning up the energy from somewhere within me, walked onto the stage.

The play was set in Russia, in a train station waiting room. I was wearing a thick fur coat as part of my costume, and was glad for the extra layer to keep me warm. The adrenaline and painkillers I'd taken half an hour before suddenly kicked in, and I began to enjoy myself. I had performed with this group of actors before and we worked well as a team. Our interaction was sharp and we remembered all our lines. No one would have guessed that our last rehearsal was about two weeks before.

The curtain came down, and the audience began clapping loudly and cheering. It seemed to have gone better than I could have hoped. I walked off the stage, and almost fell into a chair in the dressing room. Pam came backstage to find me, and hugged me tight.

'Thank you so much, Cally. I don't know what we'd have done without you,' she said.

'You're welcome, Pam. There's no way I would've let you down.'

I said goodbye to everyone, and turned to leave. I saw my boyfriend waiting in the doorway and gave him a peck on the cheek.

'The doctor said it's your fault,' I told him jokingly. 'But seriously, are you alright? I really hope you don't get glandular fever like me.'

'I'm fine,' he reassured me. I had a feeling I wouldn't be seeing him for at least a few weeks. My parents drove me home, and I collapsed into my bed, exhausted and feeling worse than ever.

To my surprise, the next day Pam phoned to speak to my mother, who brought me the good news.

'Carolyn, Mrs Saunders just rang. Guess what? You won the runner-up prize for the best actress! She's really thrilled, and asked me to tell you "well done".'

I certainly wasn't expecting that. I was really delighted to have won a prize, especially considering my state of health. I began to reflect on my conversation with the orthopaedic specialist: 'Do you do anything else except dance?'

'No … I just do a bit of drama, and I can sing.'

'Well, my advice is that you do that, then. Never dance again.'

The words pirouetted around in my head. Over and over again I heard him say:

Never dance again. Never dance again. Never dance again.

How? How could I possibly stop dancing? How could I possibly never dance again?

Dance was my life and it was everything to me. It was all I had ever dreamed of, and now I was stuck in bed with this terrible illness *and* a bad back. I certainly had plenty of time to think about my future, so I decided I needed to make plans.

If I can't be a dancer, then I'll be an actress. I'm good, maybe good enough to make it to the top. I'll study drama at a drama school or college, and then audition for films or television. I can do pantomimes at Christmas, or work in Theatre in Education.

My mind began to reel with dreams and ideas. It was the end of one dream but the beginning of another. I loved acting, and I had dreamed of a career on the stage. Now it was just a change of direction, and it all began to seem possible again.

I'll need a stage name, I thought to myself.

After several hours of thinking of hundreds of names, I found one that felt just right.

'I've got it,' I declared out loud. I imagined myself dressed in a beautiful long gown. I was at the BAFTA awards ceremony, and I heard my name being called:

'This year's award for the Best Actress goes to Dame Cally Cameron!'

Cally Cameron.

Now, that sounded good! It had the right ring to it. That was it. Cally Cameron was my new name. Nothing was going to stop me now.

A few months later I was accepted onto a BA Honours Degree course in Performing Arts at Nonington College, part of the University of Kent in Canterbury. The plan was beginning to unfold.

The first day at the university was my nineteenth birthday, 26 September 1983. I arrived with approximately 100 other new students, and settled into my room in the halls of residence. Nonington College was in a tiny village with the same name, and the college offered just two courses, Performing Arts and Physical Education.

I had opted to study for a major in drama and a minor in music. I chose voice as my main instrument, and also did lessons in piano, guitar and flute. For the first time in my life I began to enjoy academic learning. At last I was studying something that interested me, and I wanted to make the most of every minute I could.

I finished my degree in 1986, after a term's exchange programme at Eastern Michigan University, and was now ready to launch myself as a professional actress. I started to apply for acting jobs, but needed to pay my rent and living costs. I worked first as a strawberry picker, and then a runner bean packer. Next I sweated it out in McDonald's, and then worked as an omelette cook. Actually, I was the waitress at an omelette restaurant, when, without warning, the cook gave in her notice, and left. The phone rang at the restaurant, and it was the owner asking to speak to me.

'Hello, Cally, how are you?'

'Fine thanks,' I replied. 'Just a bit concerned – the cook just walked out.'

'Yes, I know,' he answered. 'That's why I'm phoning. I was wondering if you could be the omelette cook?'

'Me?' I exclaimed. 'I've never cooked an omelette in my life.'

'That's no problem,' he replied. 'I'll teach you. Omelettes are really easy,' and before I could respond, he added, 'I'm on my way to the restaurant now, and will give you a lesson. See you soon.'

So, that's how I became an omelette cook. I cooked as many as 100 omelettes a day with a variety of different fillings. Cheese, cheese and ham, chicken, mince, tomato, bacon… The list was long. I even made sweet omelettes filled with jam and cream.

Three months later, July of 1986, and I was delighted to be able to hand in my notice at the omelette restaurant. I had successfully auditioned for Playtime Theatre Company, in Kent, as one of their touring actresses. They are a small group, and at that time were performing plays in schools throughout Kent, Sussex, Surrey and

Essex. Today they also perform international tours in various countries around the world.

My first role was in *The Harmony Stone*, playing Jo Video, a crazy astronaut marooned on a strange planet. My life as a professional actress was just beginning. I could never have imagined the drama that was to follow.

Chapter Four: The Next Step

Truly my soul finds rest in God;
my salvation comes from him.
Truly he is my rock and my salvation;
he is my fortress, I will never be shaken.
(Psalm 62:1-2)

In 1987, a year later, I met a wonderful young man and fell in love. We were together for three years before deciding to get married. We had a wonderful wedding day, and a honeymoon in Kenya. Life was very good.

I was studying at Goldsmiths college in London for a postgraduate in Senior Education. I loved teaching, and felt I needed a more secure career alongside my work as an actress. My husband worked in London, and we had bought a little flat that we made our home.

I was happy and fulfilled, and we dreamed of starting a family after a few years of marriage. Things, however, were not to happen as I had imagined. We'd been married for just four months when my life fell apart. I discovered that my husband, my best friend and the love of my life, was gay. All those years we were together he had been in an on-off relationship with another man. It's difficult to find words to describe how I felt as I wandered around in a fog of grief and desperation.

How could I not have known? How could I not have seen the signs? Why has this happened to me? How am I going to survive this? I asked myself.

I didn't even know if I *wanted* to survive. I felt as if I was inside a huge, dark cave and there was no way out. There was no tunnel with a light at the end, just darkness and hopeless despair. I moved out of our pretty little flat and went to stay with some friends.

The darkness continued and I wondered if I would ever smile or feel happy again. I felt so terrible that I went to my doctor, and told him what had happened.

'I don't know if I can go on living,' I said. 'I just want to die.'

'I'm really concerned about you,' he replied kindly. 'I want you to take a mild antidepressant.'

'I don't want to take tablets for depression. What if I start relying on them, and then can't stop?'

'It'll just stop you feeling quite so depressed. When you feel better, you'll be able to stop taking it without any problem.'

I really didn't want to take this medication but knew I needed help. I had begun smoking and drinking in an attempt to dull the pain, but that hadn't made me feel any better.

I reluctantly bought the first box of pills, and after a few days they began to take effect. I felt less desperate but the darkness just wouldn't go away. The cave seemed so huge and my grief engulfed me. I felt as if there was no hope, no joy and no peace.

My doctor had also mentioned the unmentionable.

'I'm really sorry, Carolyn, but you'll need to do an HIV test. Just to make sure.'

I had been careful in relationships during my teenage years. I wanted to wait for the 'right man' and really believed I had found him. The thought of ever having to do an HIV test had never even crossed my mind.

I went to the HIV clinic, and sat in the waiting room. I looked around me and saw young men and women waiting too. I wondered what their stories were, and their reasons for being there. I felt paralysed with fear and grief.

I looked at the pile of magazines by my side, and decided to read one. I was desperate for something to occupy my mind and stop me from panicking. I flicked through the pages of a gardening magazine, and then heard my name being called.

'Carolyn,' the receptionist said. 'Please fill in this form, and then read the information.'

She handed me the form and a sheet of paper. I couldn't stop my hands from shaking as I filled in the questions, and then read the other sheet. It informed me of the help I would receive should the test result be positive.

Positive? My stomach churned, and I struggled not to scream.

The results took a few weeks to arrive. They were dark and despairing weeks of emotional torment. A strange emptiness and hopelessness engulfed me.

One day I was alone in my friends' house and cut myself accidentally while washing up. I scrubbed the washing-up bowl three times with disinfectant, mixed with my tears. I didn't know if I was HIV positive and if I was, maybe I would infect them too. It was early on in the AIDS epidemic, and I was unaware of how it was passed from one person to another.

The test result arrived, and was negative. A huge wave of relief washed over me. And then a surge of anger, and rage and hatred. I felt like I wanted to kill my husband, and had thought about killing myself. He was my best friend, and I had loved him with all my heart.

How could he have done this to me? I asked myself the same question, over and over again. I also questioned my own failures as a wife, and wondered if I could have done things differently.

I didn't realise it at the time, but during the next few weeks I believe God sent several people into my life. On various occasions I met people who invited me to a church called 'New Life'. I had heard of this church and thought it was very strange. They didn't meet in a 'church' but held their services in the local comprehensive school.

Very dodgy, I thought. *A 'church' should be a 'church' – with a steeple and a graveyard, pulpit and organ. Not a school! Very dodgy indeed.* However, the people I met seemed so kind and genuine, and I was certainly in need of a 'new life'!

One Sunday I decided to visit the 'dodgy' church. I was greeted at the door by a very kind man who made me feel welcome, and I found a seat fairly near the back of the assembly hall. I didn't want to draw any attention to my very broken self.

I looked around me. There were people of all ages arriving in the hall, and greeting each other. There were about 100 chairs set out and some brightly coloured banners with beautifully embroidered pictures and Bible verses.

After a few minutes of waiting, everyone stood up and began to sing. I was astonished to see a band made up of singers, guitarists, a keyboard player and even a drummer. The songs were lively, and the people were clapping to the rhythm of the music. They sang a few more happy songs, and then a gentler song began.

The atmosphere changed. People stopped clapping, and some even raised their hands in the air. I looked around the room, and saw that most people had their eyes shut, and seemed to know the words of the songs by heart. They were singing as if they knew God intimately, in a way I had certainly never experienced.

I knew at that moment that I needed God in my life. I had always believed in Him, but just as an old man on a cloud, powerful but distant. I knew that these people had something special, and I felt I needed it too.

After the meeting I went back to the house where I was staying. I was house-sitting for a friend who was in Australia, and was struggling with feelings of loneliness and despair. Someone had given me a little book with daily Bible readings. That night, before I went to bed, I opened the book. The Bible verse for that day seemed to leap off the page straight into my heart,

I have heard your prayer and seen your tears; I will heal you.
(2 Kings 20:5)

I cried as I read the words – tears of joy. Also tears of gratefulness that I was beginning to know God in a new way. Then came tears of pain and brokenness. A deep, deep pain that never seemed to go away.

At the next church meeting, the pastor was speaking. He was a wonderful, dedicated man of God called Ben White. He was a gifted Bible teacher, and also had a ministry of taking Bibles into China; he died a few years ago.

He was talking about a story in the Bible found in Exodus 21:5-6. It tells of masters in the olden times piercing their servant's ear with an awl. This was the way the servant proved to his master that he would be faithful to him forever. Ben was teaching how Christians should 'pierce their ear' with an awl for God. He didn't mean this literally, but in order to live their lives fully dedicated to the Lord, and serve Him forever.

The sermon was powerful, but I felt so depressed that night. I was still finding it really difficult to accept what had happened; I felt such anger and resentment within me. A man called Tom Poulson, who was one of the elders[5] of the church, and his wife, Jill, were sitting close to me. Tom noticed how sad I was, and at the end of the meeting he came over to me.

'Cally, my wife and I would love to invite you to come to our house next week. Why don't you come on Thursday evening? We can have a cup of tea and a chat.'

I was feeling so full of anguish and despair, I replied rather curtly, 'No, thank you. I don't want to. I just want to die.'

Tom looked me in the eyes and sternly but lovingly said, 'I have pierced my ear with an awl – please come to my house next Thursday.'

'Oh, OK, then,' I replied. It seemed he was very concerned, and maybe he would be able to help me.

The following Thursday I went to their house. I told them my story, and the heartache of my separation from my husband. It felt like I cried the whole time we were talking, but they were so kind and understanding. After chatting for a while – I used up almost a box of tissues – they offered to pray for me.

As I sat on their sofa, I had the most overwhelming encounter with God. I felt like I was under a waterfall of love, and a deep sense of peace filled my mind. I cried what felt like a bucketful of tears, and I felt different from ever before. As they prayed through each situation, it was as if the darkness was lifting, and I could see the light again.

When I opened my eyes and looked at my watch, I realised that we had been praying for almost two hours. It felt to me like it was just a few minutes. My head was strangely light, and I was having difficulty focusing.

---

[5] Leaders.

'Wow!' I exclaimed. 'This is really strange. I feel like I'm drunk.'

Tom explained that it was the presence of the Holy Spirit. I stood up to go home, feeling very wobbly, and walked in the direction of the front door. I was just about to leave when I remembered the packet of cigarettes in my pocket. I took them out, and placed them in Tom's hand.

'I don't need these anymore,' I said. 'I have Jesus inside me!'

I felt so clean and so full of God that I didn't want to put anything dirty inside me. I'd been smoking thirty cigarettes a day for months, but I really didn't need to smoke anymore, and haven't since.

In the following days I felt God leading me and helping me through this very difficult time. One thing I wasn't able to avoid was the subject of forgiveness. I knew I had to forgive my husband, but I didn't know how.

One day I knelt on the floor and cried out from the very depths of my soul: 'God! Please show me how to forgive him. All I feel is anger and hatred. Please teach me how to forgive.' At that moment I had a very clear vision of Jesus on the cross, and a deep awareness of my sin, of so many things that I'd done wrong in my life. It was overwhelming, and I realised that if God had forgiven me, then I also could forgive my husband. I lay on the floor and cried and prayed for several minutes. That was the beginning of a long process of forgiveness that lasted for several years.

In May of 1991 I went on holiday to Cornwall with a group from the church, and made the decision to be baptised. It was a beautiful sunny day, and the beach was crowded with families enjoying the sand and sea. Seagulls swooped in the sky above, squawking loudly, and dive-bombing the tourists. Children squealed in delight as they jumped the waves, and paddled in the sea. The sun was warm on my skin, and it felt like a good day.

I walked slowly into the water with my two friends who had agreed to baptise me. They were shivering in the freezing cold water, as we walked further and further into the sea. Soon we were up to our waists, but surprisingly I didn't feel cold. Instead the water seemed really warm, and I felt God's presence very powerfully at that moment.

Earlier that morning I had prayed this prayer:

God, I don't want my life anymore. If You're real, and I really believe You are, then You can have my life, and do what You want with me. Wherever You want to send me, I will go. Whatever You want me to do, I will do it. I give my life to You, 100 per cent. I don't want to be a Christian who goes to church on Sunday, then the rest of the week live my life as if You don't exist. If You're real, and I really believe You are, then You deserve my all.

I have discovered it is risky to pray like this as God really does hear our prayers. If we offer our lives to Him, and pray serious prayers of commitment, He will take us at our word.

A few months later I moved to Milton Keynes to start work as a senior school teacher. I wanted to get away from Kent, and make a fresh start, so I joined a church and made a new group of friends.

The following year, in 1992, I went to Mumbai (at that time called Bombay) in India. It was a two-week trip with the worship group from my church. That trip was my first encounter with real poverty, and my eyes were opened to a world that changed me deeply. I had no idea that it would be there, in India, that I would sense my first call to full-time ministry. One of my experiences during those two weeks will remain with me forever.

One evening we were invited to lead worship at a house group. We boarded a train from the centre of Mumbai, and travelled for about an hour to the outskirts of the city. We were chatting and laughing, and the journey passed by quite quickly. I had no idea that the return journey would impact me so deeply.

The meeting was joyful and exuberant. We praised and worshipped together with the Indian Christians who were so zealous and passionate for Jesus. Becoming a Christian in India is not a small commitment. They have to renounce their Muslim or Hindu faith, which often means rejection from their families, their communities and their workplace.

For them it's not just praying a short salvation prayer. It's a commitment that can lead even to death. When they make a decision to follow Jesus, they follow Him with all their heart, soul, mind and strength.[6] The courageous and beautiful people I met that night challenged me deeply, and inspired me to a higher and closer walk with God.

The meeting ended, and we said our farewells. We were tired but so grateful for the privilege of worshipping with these 'brothers' and 'sisters'. We walked to the station, boarded the train and began the return journey to the centre of Mumbai. It was late at night, and the city was beginning to sleep.

I chose a seat beside the window. I had intended to rest my head on the glass, and try to sleep for a while. It was nearly midnight, and I couldn't believe how hot it still was, even at this late hour. Perspiration dripped down my face and neck, and I fanned my face with my hand in an attempt to cool myself down.

The train rattled to a stop at each station, the passengers leaving the carriage, and walking off into the darkness. After about five or six stations we stopped once again. I peered through the dusty, dirty window of the train and couldn't believe what I was seeing.

I blinked to clear my eyes of the perspiration, but the salty sweat stung my eyes and I struggled to see. I blinked again. There were

---

[6] See Matthew 22:37.

people of all ages lying on the platform – adults, teenagers and children. It was obvious none of them were waiting for the train. They were *sleeping* on the platform. About twenty people, some alone and some huddled together. The train roared and we continued on our way. I couldn't believe that people would have to sleep in such a place. I felt so sad, and so shocked by the scene.

My sadness and shock at that moment were nothing compared to the rest of the journey. At every station the number of bodies increased. Pushing my nose against the glass I forced myself to look. As we arrived closer and closer to the centre of the city, I saw less of the platform, and more and more bodies.

Eventually, when we reached the last few stations, the platforms were no more. There was just a mass of bodies. There were hundreds and hundreds of homeless people, asleep on the platforms. The train stations were their bedroom, the platforms their beds.

I felt like my heart was breaking and stretching at the same time. I could make out the figures of adults and teenagers, and then I saw something else. At that moment I realised I was witnessing something that would change my life forever.

Tiny children of no more than two or three years of age were lying together, fast asleep in sweaty embraces. No parents nearby. Just small, vulnerable infants, all alone except for each other. The dam burst behind my eyes and tears flowed down my cheeks like a river. Tears streamed down my cheeks and neck, mixing with my perspiration and making a huge wet patch on my T-shirt.

I knew at that moment God was sharing with me a glimpse of His heart. I didn't know which nation or nations God would call me to. I just had a deep certainty that one day He would call me, and wherever He wanted to send me I promised Him I would respond to His call.

Chapter Five: Ask, Ask, Ask

I love those who love me,
and those who seek me find me.
(Proverbs 8:17)

That trip to India was a turning point in my life. I knew that serving God full-time as a missionary would require training and preparation, so I began to pray about going to Bible college.

Some years before, my godmother Peggy had died, and had left me a few hundred pounds in her will. I didn't know what to do with the money so deposited it in a savings account, for use at a later date. When I checked the account, it had gained some interest, and was just £10 more than the amount I needed to pay for Bible college. I enrolled at King's Bible College in Scotland[7] in 1993, and spent ten wonderful months studying for a diploma in Theological and Biblical Studies. It was a time of spiritual growth and learning as I soaked up the teaching, and drew closer to God.

During the first term, a pastor from Canada came to teach us about prayer. We spent a whole week learning how to use the Lord's Prayer as a model for our prayer times. He broke the prayer down

---

[7] Now located in Oxford: King's Bible College and Training Centre.

into small chunks, and the first day we learned about just the first four words, 'Our Father in heaven'.[8] The next day we looked at the words, 'hallowed be your name'.[9] We learned about the names of God, and how powerful it is to declare them in our times of prayer. The week continued, and for the first time ever I learned how to pray, and spend time in God's presence. I also learned that God wants to meet with us just as much, or even more, than we want to meet with Him. He loves it when we call on Him, and spend time in His presence.

At the end of the week the pastor gave us a challenge.

'Raise your hand if you use an alarm clock,' he said, 'and can't wake up without one.'

I lifted my hand in the air. I always use an alarm clock, and sometimes two if necessary. I can't sleep peacefully if I'm concerned my alarm won't go off for some reason, especially if something important is planned for the next day.

'I'm going to give you all a challenge,' he explained. 'Tomorrow, don't set your alarm clock and ask God to wake you up. We all agree He wants to meet with us, right? So, tomorrow, don't set your alarm and see what happens.'

See what happens, I thought to myself. *I know what will happen. I'll sleep longer than I should, and miss not only my prayer time, but breakfast as well!*

'And not only that,' he continued, 'ask God to wake you up at a really specific time. Something like 6:42 a.m.'

We all laughed out loud.

'Trust Him that He'll wake you up,' he insisted. 'He wants to meet with you so much more than you can imagine. Just trust Him.'

---

[8] Matthew 6:9.
[9] Matthew 6:9.

I'm going to try this, I thought. *I really believe God longs to meet with me. Tomorrow is Saturday. If I do oversleep I won't miss any lectures, and I can miss breakfast quite easily. I'm going to give it a try.*

That night I got into bed, turned off my alarm clock, and left the digital display shining brightly in the darkness.

Father, I love You so much, and I really want to meet with You tomorrow morning, I prayed. *Please wake me up, and...* hesitantly I asked Him, *please let it be at 6:57a.m.* I pulled my quilt up to my neck and fell into a deep sleep. It had been a wonderful week and I felt satisfyingly tired from many hours of prayer and worship.

I woke up the next morning, and instantly remembered my prayer from the night before. I turned over in bed with my eyes still shut tight.

What time would my clock show? Would it be the time I had asked for?

I laid there, my heart beginning to beat faster in anticipation. I opened my eyes. There on my bedside table the digital display on the alarm clock was showing the time, in bright green numbers.

'What?' I gasped, and grabbed the clock with both my hands. I blinked several times to make sure I wasn't dreaming. '6:57!' I exclaimed.

'Lord!' I cried out, dropping the clock and jumping out of bed. Grabbing some clothes from the wardrobe, I dressed quickly and, my heart racing, ran to the prayer room. I threw myself facedown on the floor, and burst into tears. I lay there on the floor for several minutes, in awe of what had just happened.

The creator of the universe stopped for me. Stopped the world to wake me up. How amazing is that? How incredible? Father, I love You. Thank You. Thank You so much.

I spent an hour of uninterrupted prayer and worship, praying and singing at the top of my voice. What an awesome God. What an amazing Father. I felt so loved and cherished, and left the prayer room almost floating.

So, 6:57 a.m. will always be a special time for me. It is my moment in eternity, when God woke me up, to spend time with me. Just with me.

A few weeks before I began my studies at King's Bible College I attended an evangelism conference. One of the speakers was an American evangelist called Connie Taylor. She works with YWAM[10] in the UK, and was one of the guest speakers at the conference. I was in awe of this tall, beautiful woman, with long, red hair and a fiery passion for Jesus. I scribbled down almost every word that she spoke, wanting to remember everything she was teaching.

During the coffee break I went to the toilet, and felt God speak to me. Not an audible voice, but a sense in my mind that He was asking me my deepest desire. In my head I told him the first thing that came into my mind.

I want to be discipled[11] by Connie Taylor. My next thought was: *That's crazy! That's like asking Nigel Mansell to teach me to drive racing cars.*

I looked in the mirror, brushed my hair into place and went back to the conference room. I didn't think about it again until a few weeks later when I moved to Scotland to study at King's Bible College.

A pastor from Basingstoke called Dave Marchment arrived to teach us about evangelism. I knew Dave from various conferences I had attended, and was eager to learn more from him, and his amazing

---

[10] Youth With A Mission.

[11] Discipleship is a process in which a mature Christian guides and challenges another Christian in the outworking of their faith.

experiences. I was always very impressed with his gift for evangelism, and his desire to tell people about Jesus.

One evening after dinner I asked if I could talk to him.

'Dave, it was so good to hear what you taught today. I'm really inspired by your life and your gift for evangelism. I love telling people about Jesus everywhere I go and I really want to learn more.'

'That's wonderful, Cally,' he replied.

With great embarrassment I then said, 'Dave, I know this sounds crazy, but my deepest desire is to be discipled by Connie Taylor.'

'Well, isn't that amazing!' he exclaimed. 'I had lunch with her last Sunday.'

My chin nearly dropped on the table before me, and I sat there speechless for a few moments. I realised that he not only knew her well, but he had invited her to his house for lunch. I couldn't believe it when I heard him say.

'Cally, I think that sounds like a wonderful idea. My suggestion is that you write to her. Tell her your desire to be discipled by her, and see what she says. I'll write to her as well, and tell her all about you'.

Maybe dreams really do come true, I thought. I thanked Dave and ran to my bedroom. I couldn't sleep that night for several hours, as I pondered what I should write in my letter to Connie.

The next day I wrote a short letter, telling her of my meeting with Dave. I couldn't summon up the courage to ask her to disciple me, but told her of my desire to learn, and grow as an evangelist. I posted the letter, my hands shaking as I heard it drop down inside the postbox.

A few weeks later a letter arrived for me at the Bible college. My hands shook again as I opened the envelope. It was from Connie. She wrote that she had received my letter, and also one from Dave, and was excited to hear of my desire to serve God as an evangelist. She explained that she and her husband, Andrew, were planning to go to Estonia to lead the first YWAM Discipleship Training School there.

The training was to start in September of 1994 (a few months later) and she was inviting me to take part, and be discipled by her. When I read her words I leapt into the air, dancing and crying with joy. My desire had come true. This was the most amazing opportunity and I had to take it.

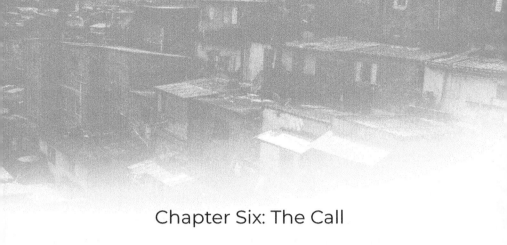

Chapter Six: The Call

If you are always trying to be normal you will never know
how amazing you can be.
Maya Angelou[12]

Sometimes I struggle with telling people that I know with absolute
certainty that God 'called' me to Brazil. I'm aware it sounds a bit
pretentious. There are so many millions of Christians in the world,
so can it really be true that God would call me? Is it possible that He
would seek me out and find me, in my bedroom in Milton Keynes,
England, and send me a personal invitation? I can say with all
honesty, I really believe He did.

It was June 1994, a few months before I was due to start the YWAM
course, and I was in my bedroom in Milton Keynes. It was a quiet
Sunday afternoon, and I was relaxing on my bed reading a Christian
magazine. My attention was drawn to an article about street children
in São Paulo, Brazil. The article explained that thousands of children
live on the streets, and are considered a terrible nuisance.

---

[12] Maya Angelou, *Rainbow in the Cloud: The Wisdom and Spirit of Maya Angelou* (New York, NY: Random House, 2014).

They sleep in doorways of banks and shops, they urinate and defecate in the streets, stealing and pickpocketing to survive. Often the police round them up and take them to shelters for homeless children, or to the youth prisons. Sometimes corrupt police even drive them out into the countryside, down lonely lanes, and murder them.

The article touched me deeply.[13] I continued reading and discovered that many of the children choose to sleep underneath the streets, in the tunnels and sewers. They sleep there to escape from paedophiles or the corrupt police, as they feel safer there and 'protected' from harm. However, nothing can protect them from the violent tropical storms in the summer months. Torrential rains quickly fill up the sewers and the tunnels at night, and they drown as they sleep.

As I read this I began to weep, uncontrollably, for several minutes. A deep sadness invaded my heart, and over the next few days I felt a longing to try to do something to help.

As the days and weeks went by, the images of drowning children in São Paulo frequently came back to my mind. I remembered that night on the train in Mumbai, when I saw the children asleep on the station platforms. A sense of indignation rose up within me that children all over the world are living on the streets. Every day I prayed for those children, without knowing their names, with a profound grief that led me to weep over and over again.

I felt so touched by the plight of these children I began to ask God if He wanted me to go to São Paulo. If only I could rescue these children from such terrible living conditions. I remember saying to God, 'If I can just rescue just one child from the streets, my life will have been worth living. But, God, please help me to rescue many, many more.'

---

[13] Sadly I cannot recall details of the source.

I felt God was calling me to go. However, I really wanted to be sure it was Him who was calling me, and not just my imagination or an emotional reaction. I had a real sense that I would serve God abroad in the future. However, I wanted to go where He was sending me. If it were to be Brazil or China, France or Afghanistan, or any other nation, then I would go. I really wanted to serve Him, so I prayed and asked for a sign: *Father, if You want me to go to Brazil,* I prayed, *then please give me such a clear sign that I will* know *it's Your will. Lord, I don't want to get it wrong. Please show me Your will.*

A few weeks later I visited friends in Kent, and was walking along the seafront, still praying for my sign. Actually, I was crying and praying, asking God to confirm this deep longing within me to go to São Paulo.

I stopped and looked up at the sky.

God, just write it in the clouds, I prayed. *'Cally, go to Brazil.' You can do that, God. I know You can.*

I stood there for a few minutes watching the sky, believing God could form the clouds into a message for me if He wanted to. The wind was moving the clouds slowly across the sky, but nothing appeared. I glanced behind me, and saw several dog-walkers also staring at the sky, in the same direction as I had been looking. I lowered my head, and hurried along the promenade, pretending everything was completely normal.

After a few hundred metres I decided to stop walking, and crossed the road to buy something from the corner shop. I knew my eyes were red from crying, and I was embarrassed to look at the shopkeeper's face. I quickly paid for a newspaper without making eye contact, and hurried out of the store.

As I looked up to cross the road, I stopped. A car drove past me, and then a bus. I strained to see what I thought I had seen. There, on the other side of the road, directly in front of me, was a skip. I felt as though my heart leapt into my throat as I realised what I was seeing. There was nothing special about the skip. It was yellow and old and full of rubbish. However, something very special was written across the side of the skip in large red capital letters. BRASIL.

There was my sign. Not in the clouds, but on the side of a skip. I stared at it and saw the word BRASIL. Nothing else was written there. No telephone number or address of the company who owned the skip. Just BRASIL. And written in Portuguese. With an 'S'.

I stopped crying, and began to laugh. There, all by myself in front of the skip, laughing with joy, knowing with absolute certainty that God had spoken to me. What an amazing moment. I was overwhelmed with the reality that God, the creator of this universe, had placed a skip just where I needed to see it, just for me, and to confirm my call to Brazil. That was a very special moment, and one I will remember forever.

However, I have to confess, I wasn't satisfied with just one sign. I needed to be *really* sure and asked God to confirm it again. It was the summer holidays of 1994, and I had been invited to lead the children's work at a church summer camp in Devon.

The day I arrived I took some time to pray and commit my week to God. I was going to be working hard teaching the children, and I wanted them to have fun and grow in their relationship with the Lord. I also asked God to confirm my call to Brazil, *again.* I prayed, *Lord, if You want me to go to Brazil, please get someone to say the word 'Brazil' to me in the next three days.*

Simple. Just the word 'Brazil'.

The next day, after lunch, some people from the church were sitting on the campsite, drinking tea. It was a lovely sunny day, and everyone was chatting and enjoying being together, and I was beginning to make some new friends. Suddenly, one of the women invited me to tell them my testimony.[14] I told them a few details of my life, and of how I had met God through the break-up of my marriage. Then, at the end, I told them of a prophecy I had received.

'Last year, when I was at King's Bible College a pastor came to teach us about prophecy.[15] He didn't know the students at the Bible college at all, but spoke to each of us in turn, and we were all excited to hear what this godly man would say.

'When it was my turn my heart began to beat so fast I thought it was going to burst out of my chest. He began by saying he felt God had shown him a picture[16] of a red and green saucer. He sensed that God was saying that this picture represented me, and my life. The saucer had many intricate designs, and he felt God showing him that I am very artistic and creative.

'However, the prophecy didn't end there. He also felt that God had shown him there was a cup for my saucer, but that the cup was very different from me. It was blue and yellow and represented my future husband. He would be completely different from me, but God would put us together at the right time.'

'Ah, that is so lovely,' one of the women said.

'Yes, it was so special. He said that he also felt God was showing him that I was brokenhearted, and that in my inmost self I was afraid

---

[14] The story of how I became a Christian.

[15] Prophecy is a spiritual gift given by God to communicate to His people. Peter, one of Jesus' disciples, wrote about prophecy to the early Christians in 2 Peter 1:20-21: 'Above all, you must understand that no prophecy of Scripture came about by the prophet's own interpretation of things. For prophecy never had its origin in the human will, but prophets, though human, spoke from God as they were carried along by the Holy Spirit.'

[16] God sometimes speaks to His people using 'pictures' or images.

of being hurt again. However, God was preparing me, and at the right time would bring this man into my life.'

Everyone thanked me for sharing, and made encouraging comments about how good it was that I had found God, and that they would pray for me to meet my 'cup'.

Remember, the day before I had asked God to get someone to say the word 'Brazil' to me, in the following three days? A few minutes later something else happened that changed the direction of my life. A man called John Hallsworth looked at me across the circle of people, and said, 'Cally, have you ever thought of going to Brazil?'

I froze as I heard his words, and a shiver went down my spine.

'Why did you say that?' I asked.

'Well, their colours are blue and yellow, aren't they?' he replied.

The strange thing is that the colours of the Brazilian flag are predominantly *green* and yellow, not *blue* and yellow. However, John explained he was thinking of the Brazilian football team colours, which are indeed blue and yellow, the colours of my 'cup'.

I believe God supernaturally used John that day to give me one more, huge sign that He was indeed calling me to Brazil. I went back to my room, my mind reeling with the reality that God had spoken clearly once again. Now I felt sure that Brazil would be the nation where I would serve God. I even felt sure it would be for the rest of my life.

It seemed that possibly I would find my *cup* in Brazil. Could the husband God was preparing for me be waiting for me there? Was I ready to step out in faith, and be married again? Was I prepared to love again? Was I prepared to be hurt again?

I told John and his wife, Eileen, a few years later that I was moving to Brazil to answer God's call. John was so encouraged to have been part of the story that they committed to supporting me financially every month, and still faithfully support me and pray for me to this day.

Chapter Seven: Lessons to Be Learned

Whatever you want to do, if you want to be great at it, you have to love it and be able to make sacrifices for it.

Maya Angelou[17]

Soon after the camp, I left for Estonia to take part in the YWAM Discipleship Training School, to be discipled by Connie Taylor. My few months in Estonia were challenging, and an intense time of learning and growth. Everything I had learned at Bible school seemed to move from my head down to my heart. I learned about God's heart as our Father, and fully understood, for the first time, just how much God loves me.

Connie was my small group leader and I spent every available moment with her, soaking up all that she had to teach me. She was an inspiration to me in so many ways, and became a very special friend. She and Andrew have supported me financially every month ever since. Missionaries supporting a missionary – awesome!

Our first challenge was just a few days after we arrived, when the ferry named *The Estonia* sank during a storm in the Baltic Sea. More

---

[17] Frank Johnson, *The Very Best of Maya Angelou: The Voice of Inspiration* (Scotts Valley, CA: CreateSpace Independent Publishing Platform, 2014).

than 850 passengers and crew died in the tragedy. The ship was the pride of the Estonian nation, and it was a huge tragedy for such a small country. We felt moved to pray and intercede for the families of those who had died. It was a very difficult time, as most of the students at the school were Estonians and lost friends or loved ones in the disaster.

The living conditions at the YWAM training school were also very challenging. It was the first Discipleship Training School in Estonia, and a wonderful building was being built to accommodate the students and staff. However, it wasn't finished in time for the start of our school, and so we were found alternative accommodation. Plan B was a wooden summerhouse in the middle of a forest.

Two weeks after we all moved in, there was a knock at the front door. One of the Estonian students opened it, and we saw a middle-aged man with a long beard and a serious expression on his face. There were six of us from the United Kingdom, and we had no idea why the man had arrived, or what he was saying. A rather heated conversation began between him and the Estonian student, and a few minutes later he left. The student turned to us all with a forlorn look on her face.

'What happened?' I asked. 'Who was that?'

'It was the owner of the house,' she replied. 'He came to inform us that he's turning off the water.'

Oh, that's not too bad, I thought, imagining it was just for that day. *Maybe he needs to mend a pipe or something.*

'When's he turning it back on?' I asked.

'In the spring,' she replied. 'Winter is setting in. He said he has to turn the water off now, or the pipes might burst.'

We all looked at each other in dismay. What were we going to do? We were not only living in a wooden summerhouse in winter, but now we had no water!

A plan was put into action. Every day Connie's husband, Andrew, drove a few miles to a petrol station, and there we filled up various plastic bottles from a tap. I was aware that the training school would be a challenge, and a character-building experience, so I tried not to complain at this inconvenience. One day, however, I couldn't control myself and expressed my frustration to Andrew. We were returning to the summerhouse, the car full of bottles of water.

'Andrew, this is ridiculous. How are we going to survive like this for the next three months?' I exclaimed.

His reply touched me deeply.

'Cally, we're experiencing what a huge percentage of the world experience every day of their lives. Millions of people have no access to water. They have to collect it every day, not just for three months.'

His words stopped me in my tracks. I realised how blessed I am to have always been able to simply turn on a tap and have access to running water. I asked God to forgive me for my complaining spirit, and made a decision to have a better attitude.

After arriving with the water, the bottles were then distributed for use. Some were used for cooking, others for washing up, some for cleaning and the rest for 'showers'. We were encouraged to wash every two or three days, with just a couple of saucepans of water.

My biggest problem was the toilet, as I often needed to use it in the middle of the night. The inside toilet was out of bounds as there was no water for flushing. The nearest 'convenience' was a walk through the forest, in complete darkness, to a wooden shack with a hole in the ground.

It definitely was character-building stuff, especially in sub zero temperatures, and certainly raised my faith levels. I left the house almost every night, praying for protection from wild animals and lurking attackers. As soon as I returned to my bed, I thanked God for another safe expedition to the forest toilet.

One night I was in the shack, hovering above the hole, when suddenly everything went black. I grabbed my torch and shook it vigorously. I realised, to my dismay, that the batteries were flat. At that moment I also realised that forests at night in the middle of nowhere are pitch black. There is absolutely no light from houses, lampposts, or anything. It was so dark I couldn't see a thing, not even my hand in front of my face.

Just as I was about to panic, and begin shouting for help, a Bible verse came into my mind:

> Your word is a lamp for my feet, a light on my path.[18]

Over and over again the words repeated:

> Your word is a lamp for my feet, a light on my path.
> Your word is a lamp for my feet, a light on my path.
> Your word is a lamp for my feet, a light on my path.

A deep sense of peace overwhelmed me, and I walked very slowly but confidently back to the summerhouse, in total darkness, feeling no fear at all. It was an amazing moment as I sensed the presence of God so powerfully, giving me total peace and confidence.

The most frustrating thing for me was living in the summerhouse with a group of Christians and not being able to tell anyone about Jesus. I decided to prepare myself. I asked one of the Estonian students to teach me about six short phrases in the Estonian language. I needed simple phrases that I could use to tell someone about Jesus, if I ever got the opportunity. They were very difficult to memorise so I

---

[18] Psalm 119:105.

wrote them on a piece of paper, and every night laid in bed repeating them to myself.

One evening Connie informed me that she was going to the capital city of Tallinn to speak at a church meeting, and invited me to go with her. I was so excited to be 'let out' for a few hours, and practised my six phrases over and over again, just in case I had the chance to use them.

After the church meeting, we stopped to fill the car with petrol and then enjoyed an ice cream together. It was cold outside, but inside the car it was warm. Our breath steamed up the glass and after a few minutes we could hardly see through the windows. It was so good to chat to Connie, and learn from her close and intimate walk with God.

After a few minutes a strange figure appeared beside the car door. I could just make out the shape of a person, with their arm stretched out, as if asking for money. Instantly I grabbed my purse, and found some coins.

I jumped out of the car and saw it was an old man, dressed in a shabby overcoat, with a long beard and a wild head of hair. I looked into his eyes and, with the most loving expression I could possibly muster, said my six Estonian phrases. I told him Jesus loved him, and that God had a plan for his life. He lifted his arms and started making gestures. He pointed to his ears, and made some strange muffled sounds, shaking his head, trying to communicate with me.

I realised, to my dismay, that he was deaf. He hadn't heard any of my well-rehearsed phrases. In fact, he hadn't heard a word I had said. I pressed the coins into his hands, and smiled at him, not knowing whether to laugh or to cry.

As we drove back to the summerhouse, laughing at my experience, I reflected on what had just happened. I accepted that this was a time to receive. It was a precious time to learn and grow, not to struggle and be frustrated. This was a time to surrender my life to God, and allow Him to do all that He wanted to do in me. I knew that at the right time He would set me free, and I would be able to tell many, many people about the love of Jesus. And hopefully they would be able to hear me!

Chapter Eight: Divine Intervention

Ah, Sovereign LORD, you have made the heavens and the earth by
your great power and outstretched arm.
Nothing is too hard for you.
(Jeremiah 32:17)

I am fascinated by the way our brains work, enabling us to learn new
languages. However, some languages are definitely more difficult
to learn than others, and I discovered this in Estonia. No words in
Estonian seemed to relate to English, French or Latin, the languages
I had learned at school. Years later when I was trying to learn
Portuguese in Brazil there were at least a few words I could decipher.
Estonian, however, I had to learn off by heart, repeating phrases like
a parrot.

During the first three months at the training school I did manage
to learn enough for a basic conversation, but not much more. I never
imagined I would experience an incredible 'language' miracle while
in Estonia.

At the end of the lecture phase of the Discipleship Training School,
we were divided into teams, and sent out to work in different towns.
My team was led by a young Estonian couple called Erik and Evelin.

Two weeks before we were due to start, we went for a visit to see our accommodation and the town.

I was excited about this new challenge. We would be working with the church, leading activities with the children and teaching English to groups of students in the local schools. Two of our team members would be our translators, so we wouldn't have too many problems with communication. I was full of faith from the lecture phase, and eager to put into action all I had learned.

The day after our arrival at Erik's house he announced that he was going to buy some pigs for his father, and asked if anyone wanted to accompany him. I was anxious to learn more about the culture and had never bought pigs before, so agreed to go with him.

We said goodbye to the team and set off in his van. It was very cold and snowy, and the journey was long and slow. The temperature was sub zero; it was colder than I had ever experienced.

After about half an hour we stopped at a farm and bought two little piglets. Erik placed them in a sack, closed it tightly with a rope, and we continued our journey to his parents' house. I never imagined piglets could squeal so loudly. They rolled around noisily on the floor of the van as the sack moved back and forth. I was extremely relieved when we arrived at our destination.

Erik's parents were delighted to see us, and his mother insisted on serving us hot tea and cake. I was grateful for the opportunity to warm myself by their open fire, but all too quickly it was time to make our way home. We presented Erik's father with the pigs, and set off.

The road was straight and the landscape bare. There were no shops or restaurants along the way, just miles and miles of snowy road. I wondered what God was going to do in this place, and how we could best serve Him to bless these needy people.

A few minutes after our departure Erik calmly announced, 'Sorry to tell you this, but the van is almost out of petrol.'

My heart sank as I stared at the long road ahead of us. I wondered what time we would arrive home that day, if at all.

'What do we do if the petrol does run out?' I asked.

'We have to wait for a kind person to stop and tow us to the next petrol station.'

That didn't sound very hopeful. I didn't relish the thought of sitting on the side of a deserted road in the freezing cold. However, if we did need to sit in the van on the roadside and wait, my faith was sufficient to know we would survive. I certainly didn't want to die before we had even started our work in that place.

I didn't have long to contemplate these thoughts as moments later the van's engine began to splutter, and we ground to a halt on the hard shoulder. Erik suggested we prayed for help to arrive, so we prayed together and asked God to rescue us. I really hoped that help would arrive soon. It was so cold, and now we couldn't use the van engine to keep us warm.

About thirty minutes later a car full of young men and women stopped and asked if we needed help. Erik explained that we had run out of petrol, so they offered to tow us to the nearest petrol station. I felt a surge of relief within me, and began to dream of a lovely hot cup of tea on our arrival home.

There was just one problem. Their petrol tank was almost empty and no one was sure if the next petrol station was close by. They tied on the towrope, and with hope in our hearts we all set off. I held my breath, wondering if at any moment we would have to stop again and wait for *two* kind motorists to help us – we would need one to tow our van and the other to tow the car. I began to relax, confident that a petrol station would appear around the next bend. The barren landscape continued, however, uninterrupted by anything except the car and our van.

Surely there will be one around the next bend, maybe? Or the next, I thought to myself.

Erik braked suddenly, almost crashing into the bumper of the young people's car in front. I felt that sinking feeling when everything seems to be going differently from how you had hoped. Our worst fears had just happened. Their car had also run out of petrol, and our return home was looking more complicated by the minute.

Erik jumped out of the van to go and talk to the young people. I joined him, smiling and pretending I was totally relaxed with the whole situation. Actually, I was beginning to feel really concerned. I was worried about the petrol, or the lack of it. But I was more worried about the extreme cold I was feeling and the lack of sensation in any of my toes.

I knew if I had to wait there in the cold for much longer I was at risk of hypothermia, and began to pray fervently for a solution. I chided myself for not being equipped with the fur-lined boots the others were wearing. I now realised these were a basic requirement for winter in Estonia.

If I live to tell this tale I will buy myself some proper boots, I promised myself.

God certainly had mercy on my toes that day as only a few minutes later a car appeared, and the motorist stopped to help. There was no recovery service at that time in Estonia, but fortunately they are a generous people willing to help each other, whatever the inconvenience.

Erik and the young people explained to the motorist what had happened, and the plan was put in place. The motorist would tow the young people's car, and Erik would go with them. They would fill up their car and then give him a lift back with a can of petrol.

However, there was just one more problem. Their car was full, and so one of the young people would need to give up their seat to make room for Erik. A young woman called Karina offered to stay with me in the van, and the others set off for the petrol station.

She was a pretty, dark-haired girl, in her mid-twenties. Her eyes were jet black, and her skin so white it was almost transparent. She seemed friendly, and quite content to wait with me in in the van. I was also happy to have company, as I would have felt rather uneasy waiting there all by myself.

We began to chat, and I used up all my basic Estonian conversation within the first few minutes. I was very relieved, therefore, when she spoke and understood English. We were able to communicate quite easily, and she told me her story.

She had married very young and soon after, gave birth to a son. Life was good and, although she was quite poor, she and her husband were happy. However, tragically, when her son was just three years old, her husband died in an accident. Tears began to roll down her cheeks as she told me of her pain and sadness at losing her husband so young; also of how difficult it was to raise her son alone, and with little help. She wiped her face repeatedly as the tears flowed, and I sensed she needed this opportunity to speak of her grief.

I offered to pray for her and she accepted. She cried some more as I prayed, and afterwards thanked me for listening. I explained I would be returning with the team later that month, and she gave me her address to meet up on our arrival. She said she would be interested in attending the activities we would be running with the church. I hoped she would come to know Jesus through our meeting.

Erik arrived about forty-five minutes later, armed with a large canister of petrol, and soon after we were able to resume our journey. I hugged Karina goodbye, and promised to visit as soon as I arrived back in the town at the end of the month. My toes began to defrost as the engine slowly warmed the van, and I began to dream again of a hot cup of tea. I felt grateful for that short time I was able to spend with Karina. Praise God she could speak and understand English, and we were able to chat and pray together. I looked forward to meeting her again soon.

We arrived at Erik's house, and told the team of our adventures. They all laughed at my story of the squealing pigs, and we praised God together that we had made it home. I warmed my feet by the radiator, and enjoyed the tingling sensation of my toes returning to normal temperature.

I sipped my hot, sweet tea slowly and gratefully. I thanked God for sending such kind people to help us, and reflected on how He had taken care of every detail that day. I also prayed that I would be like the Estonians, always available to help others, whatever the inconvenience. I wondered what else God had in store for me in that place.

Two weeks later we were ready for the outreach phase. The sketches and songs were rehearsed, and the dances polished for performance. We set off to Erik and Evelin's house once again, eager to share our love for the Lord. We were full of expectation for new experiences and a challenging time, as a team and as individuals. I longed for an opportunity to meet Karina again, and soon after our arrival I set off to find her apartment.

I climbed the outside wooden stairs of the apartment block and noticed the grey and shabby walls, with paint peeling off the doors. I rang the doorbell and waited. My heart beat fast as I remembered our previous meeting. I was anxious to rekindle our friendship and invite her to our church activities.

After a few moments Karina opened the door, and a huge smile spread across her face. I could tell she remembered me. I hugged her tightly, and said excitedly, 'Hello, Karina, it's so good to see you again. How are you?'

'Hello,' she said. Then, to my immense surprise, her expression changed and she seemed confused. She appeared not to understand what I had just said.

I helped her out saying, 'Karina, we met on the side of the road, and we talked? Do you remember?'

She smiled her sweet smile, shook her head, and then said with a little embarrassment, 'English no. No speak English.'

Now it was my turn to be confused. Was this the same Karina? Was I dreaming? Had we not talked that day for forty-five minutes, mostly in English, and were able to communicate quite easily? I tried to understand, my mind reeling, wondering if I really had understood what she had told me that day. Her marriage. The accident. Her son. I tried again, not wishing to embarrass her, but desperate to understand her confusion.

'Karina, you do speak English. That day, we talked, you told me your story.'

Once again she insisted, 'English no. No speak English.'

Breaking the awkwardness, I hugged her and laughed, and spoke a few words in Estonian to encourage her. I managed to tell her the day and the time of the activities at the church the following week, and that I hoped she would take part. I certainly intended to sign her up for the English classes!

To this day I still don't know what happened. Did she speak to me in Estonian, and the Holy Spirit enabled me to understand, as if she was speaking English? Or did the Holy Spirit supernaturally enable her to speak in English, and that's why I was able to understand? Or maybe the Holy Spirit enabled me to speak in Estonian, thinking I was speaking in English? I have no idea. I just know that Karina came along to the church and the English classes, and we had an opportunity to share our faith with her. I pray that one day, when we meet in heaven, all will be revealed!

Living and working in other nations has taught me how essential it is to learn the language, even for short-term visits or missions. When we speak someone else's language it breaks down barriers, forges relationships, and shows our commitment to that nation and its people.

During my last week in Estonia I went to a supermarket with one of my English friends from the training school. She bought a bottle of fizzy drink, but was unable to open it. We stood in the queue, waiting to pay, and discussing what to do.

The Estonian man in front of us saw our concern and instantly took out a bottle opener from his pocket. Quickly he opened the bottle, and gave it back to my friend. I smiled and thanked him in Estonian.

'Oh, you speak Estonian?' he asked, surprised.

'Just a little,' I replied. 'I'm English.'

'What are you doing here?'

'We're helping at the church.'

To my amazement his eyes filled with tears. Overcome with emotion he explained, 'I have lived in this country for fifty-five years. I've never heard a foreigner speak to me in my own language. Thank you so much.'

Choking back the tears I took his hands and replied, '*Jeesus armastab sind.*' ('Jesus loves you.')

A tear ran down his cheek, and he said, 'Thank you. Thank you so much.'

I made a decision that day that wherever God took me I would make a concerted effort to learn the language, and try to speak it as fluently as possible. My deep desire is to convey the love of God wherever I go, and that day I learned an important lesson. Learning someone's language is like building a bridge between you and that person. If we don't build that bridge it is so much more difficult to communicate. God uses us when we make the effort to speak someone else's language, and even does miracles when we least expect them!

Chapter Nine: Going Home

Do what you can, with what you've got, where you are.
Squire Bill Widener (attributed to Theodore Roosevelt)[19]

A very strange thing happened during the YWAM Discipleship Training School. I began to feel acutely homesick for Milton Keynes, and wanted to go back there and work with my home church. I prayed about it, and felt God was leading me to serve the church until it was the right time to leave for Brazil. I firmly believe that we need to learn to serve God in our home church first, before we try to serve Him anywhere else.

'I've been praying,' I told my pastor. 'I feel it's right to stay in Milton Keynes until God moves me on, and I'd like to help the church and the city in some way.'

I had a real desire to reach out to the children of Milton Keynes, and wanted to use drama and singing. I was good friends with the head teacher of a Middle School where my church met every Sunday, and where I was a school governor, so I talked to him about my idea.

---

[19] Theodore Roosevelt, *An Autobiography* (New York, NY: Charles Scribner's Sons, 1920).

'I want to lead assemblies in the schools, teaching about Christianity in a fun and relevant way. I can use sketches, songs and games. I'm going to call it "Signpost for Schools". What do you think?'

He loved the idea and we performed our first assembly together at the school, which was a roaring success. The children loved to see their head teacher performing, especially playing the role of God.

He then talked to the head teacher of the First School on the same estate, and I began leading assemblies there and at other schools too, one day a week. The rest of the week I worked as a supply teacher. It was just me and my guitar to begin with. Then I invited a young man from my church, who was a very talented actor and singer, to work with me. We wrote all our own material, and soon were working in many of the schools.

After a few months I talked to my pastor again, and explained that it was becoming difficult to pay my bills. I was now working more days for 'Signpost for Schools' than as a supply teacher. He said he would talk to the church members and ask if they would be willing to support this work. Several friends started supporting me monthly with £10, £20 or more, and this was the beginning of my support base. Some of those friends still support me today, more than twenty-five years later.

I learned the importance of building a support base, financially and for prayer. I don't receive a fixed salary for my work here in São Paulo, but am supported by faithful friends and churches. Without these people and their prayers, it would be impossible to do what I do.

When I was leading 'Signpost for Schools' sometimes we needed an extra actor. A member of the church, a self-employed man, joined us for some of the presentations, which was wonderful. Another couple also joined the team, performing their excellent puppet shows based on Bible stories. We had so much fun devising the sketches and writing the songs. Sometimes we were invited to teach lessons, too, especially on the themes of Easter and Christmas.

Years later I spoke at a youth event in Milton Keynes, and a teenage girl came to speak to me afterwards.

'Cally, you won't remember me, but I remember you,' she said. 'You came to my school and taught a lesson about Easter. You talked about Jesus, and the cross, and the real meaning of Easter. That night I gave my life to Jesus. I talked to my mum, and she also gave her life to Him. Now my brother has started going to church with us too.'

What a blessing. I knew we were sowing many seeds, but I had no idea if any had borne fruit. This young girl's testimony of how she and her family had been impacted through just one lesson, made me so grateful.

I continued in this work until 1999, when I left Milton Keynes and moved to Brazil. 'Signpost for Schools' continued for ten more years, working in about forty schools, leading assemblies for more than 10,000 children a month. I often wonder how many of those children who heard the message of Jesus are now Christians, and impacting their world for Christ.

The five years between my 'call' in 1994 and my departure for Brazil in 1999 were a time of waiting and preparation. I was desperate to go to Brazil and begin my work there. However, I knew I couldn't just walk away from 'Signpost for Schools' so I did as much as I could to leave it running well.

I rented out my house, sold or gave away most of my belongings, and set off to Brazil. Most of my friends who supported me in 'Signpost for Schools' agreed to continue supporting me, and my life was now in two suitcases and the hands of God.

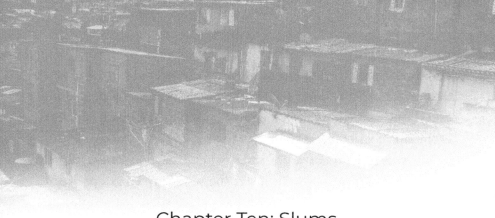

Chapter Ten: Slums

As long as poverty, injustice and gross inequality persist in our world, none of us can truly rest.

Nelson Mandela[20]

My first place of work when I arrived in São Paulo in 1999 was in a *favela*. The word '*favela*' in Portuguese means 'a weed', and is a good illustration for the way a slum begins and then expands. Usually, one or two little shacks appear seemingly out of nowhere, on unused land. In a few days or weeks there are ten shacks, then twenty, then 100, and so on, spreading out of control, just like weeds. Some *favelas* are so large they are like small towns and have thousands of inhabitants.

I discovered that *favelas* are rated from one star to five star, ironically just like hotels. In one-star *favelas* the residents live in shacks or lean-tos made of wood or cardboard, often built precariously over the sewage river below. They have no proper roads or sanitation and usually not even running water. They are rat-infested with piles of stinking rubbish, to the delight of the flies and mosquitoes which

---

[20] Address by Nelson Mandela for the 'Make Poverty History' Campaign, London, United Kingdom, 2005, http://www.mandela.gov.za/mandela_speeches/2005/050203_poverty.htm (accessed 19.5.20).

also dwell there. In the rainy seasons these *favelas* suffer the most as the torrential rains flood the shacks unmercifully. The people lose everything, sometimes even their lives, taken by surprise by the force of the storm and the power of the rain.

The two-star *favelas* are a little better. The houses are slightly sturdier and are usually built *beside* the sewage river, as opposed to directly over it. Normally the *favelas* are so crowded that people build their houses with several storeys to accomodate married offspring or elderly parents. Some dwellings have as many as five storeys, precariously balanced one on top of the other.

The three-star and four-star *favelas* are progressively better and the five-star *favelas* have proper roads and sturdy houses built of bricks. There is a proper sewage system, running water and electricity. However, this is pirated illegally through a series of pipes and wires from the main electricity and water source in the street. As a result, no one living in a *favela* has to pay electricity or water bills.

There are, however, disadvantages, as many fires occur every year in *favelas*, due to the faulty wiring. Hundreds of people die or lose their homes and their belongings, as the fires rage uncontrollably from one shack to the next. The fire service is usually hampered by almost impossible access and a group of angry residents trying desperately to save the little they have.

Today the *favelas* in São Paulo are called 'comunidades' or 'communities'. It's an attempt at offering *favela* residents some kind of dignity. It's so much more desirable to say you live in a 'community' than a place referring to a weed.

The name may have changed, but the *favelas*, however, haven't. They are some of the poorest and most dangerous places in the world. Brazil is referred to as the nation with the greatest disparity between rich and poor, and it is easy to understand why.

A startling fact is that often the most luxurious apartments are situated right beside the poorest of *favelas*. One particular example is in an area called Paraisópolis (taken from the word 'paradise') where the apartments are so ostentatious they even have swimming pools on their balconies. Literally metres away, the *favela* has grown so large it now has approximately 100,000 inhabitants. It sprawls out beneath the apartment blocks with thousands of poverty-stricken families living in the shadow of the most luxurious of apartments.

Construction companies have come to a good *solution* in some areas of the city. *Favelas* in sight of luxury shopping centres, office blocks or hotels are conveniently *hidden* behind an apartment block. This helps the rich to avoid the daily confrontation of a slum, or the reality of families living in extreme poverty. It also helps the construction companies sell their properties as their clients may be wary of choosing that area if the *favela* is glaringly conspicuous.

In recent years the government has built many tower blocks in place of the *favelas*. They bulldoze the *favela*, and move the residents into the tower blocks. They are basic dwellings, but are owned by the residents, and are certainly safer and more dignified than the *favelas*. However, there are many problems associated with these tower blocks.

Little or nothing is done to address why the people are living in a *favela* in the first place. The sad reality is that the horizontal *favelas* are simply converted to vertical *favelas*. The problems with drugs, violence and unemployment continue. Often the tower blocks are built on the outskirts of the city, where the residents are far from work, shops and schools.

Another problem is that the residents have to pay condominium charges as well as electricity and water bills. They're not accustomed to this and often don't have the money to keep up with the payments. As a result, many sell their apartments and move back into a *favela*.

A few years ago, I visited some families living in tower blocks in the north of São Paulo. I arrived to find the road in front of the apartments blocked with burning tyres, and hundreds of very angry residents in the middle of the road. The police had arrived and were standing in a row with their rifles pointing in the direction of the protesters. I felt like I'd arrived in the middle of a war zone.

Larissa saw me first. She was eleven years old, and the daughter of one of the families.

'*Tia, Tia*,' she shouted, a look of panic on her face. ('*Tia*' is Portuguese for 'Aunty' and a term of endearment used by children for adults in Brazil). 'Come quickly, follow me.'

'What's happening?' I asked her mother, who had arrived with the three other families.

'We've had no water for six days. All the residents are protesting,' she explained.

'Follow us!' Larissa and the other families began to run in the direction of the apartments, right into the firing line of the police.

What are they doing? I thought. *We're going to get shot!*

'Larissa, wait!' I shouted. 'Can't we go another way?'

Everyone stopped running, and Larissa pointed to the alternative route. It was across a swamp-like wasteland, and so much further than crossing the firing line. I'd been suffering with terrible pain in my feet for over a year, and didn't fancy going the long way.

'We can't go that way, *Tia*, it's too far, follow me,' Larissa shouted.

'OK, let's go for it,' I replied, and we ran along the side of the road for about fifty metres. Suddenly Larissa grabbed my hand, and pulled me across the road, right in front of the firing line. We all lifted our arms and waved at the police officers, screaming for them not to shoot.

My friend and her seven-year-old daughter, Sueli, had come with me that day. They ran alongside me and the families, panting out of breath as they tried to keep up. Sueli's face was pale, and she had a look of terror in her eyes.

'Don't be scared, Sueli,' I shouted. 'This is what being a missionary is like.' Her mum laughed nervously, and we all ran into the apartment block.

'This is terrible,' I said. 'Six days with no water at all. How many people live here?'

'There are 6,000 residents living in these tower blocks,' Larissa's mother replied. 'People are losing their patience. It's so difficult to live with no water.'

I remembered Andrew's words to me during the training school in Estonia, 'Cally, we're experiencing what a huge percentage of the world experience every day of their lives. Millions of people have no access to water.'

I felt so sad for those families that day. The poor in São Paulo suffer terribly, and it's so unjust the way they are treated. Despite their suffering most are hard-working and dedicated people, often waking up in the early hours of the morning to arrive at work. I am always shocked to see the buses full at six o'clock in the morning, with people travelling long distances to the other side of the city.

I am also always impressed when I see a *favela* resident leaving for work, dressed in a suit or smart clothes. They may live in a slum, but they're determined to work hard and succeed in life. Their dream is to one day leave that slum and buy their own home. I have been so blessed to see many slum-dwellers moving out of poverty and achieving their dreams. It isn't easy, but it is possible.

Chapter Eleven: Present from Heaven

Do not be anxious about anything, but in every situation, by prayer
and petition, with thanksgiving, present your requests to God.
(Philippians 4:6)

My first place of work in São Paulo was in what I consider to be
a two-star *favela*. Some of the shacks had running water, but many
didn't, and most were built over or beside the sewage river. It was also
extremely dangerous, and there were nine people murdered during
my first week.

On my second day, I arrived in the *favela* and was greeted by some
of the children I had met the day before.

'*Tia, Tia,* look, there's a dead man,' one of the children said. I didn't
understand Portuguese at that time but I am fairly certain that was
what they said. I shuddered as I saw his body lying there, half-covered
with an old blanket, and blood trickling from his head. I wondered
who he was, and what had happened.

The children managed to explain through gestures that he had
been shot just a few minutes earlier. A crowd had gathered to look,
and what shocked me most was the reaction of the children. It just
seemed to be so normal to be looking at someone dead on the ground.

I wondered how many more dead bodies I would come across in the next few months or years.

It was in this *favela* that I began my work, visiting the families, teaching English and helping in the church. It was there that I learned to speak Portuguese, and where I experienced the supernatural protection and provision of God on many different occasions.

Looking back, I can see many times in my life when God responded to my need in what I consider to be a supernatural way. People who don't believe in God explain these moments as coincidences. I like to call them 'Christ-incidences'. They happen in my life too often and with too much precision to be merely coincidental.

One of those times was during my first week, when I was visiting families in the *favela*. I was standing in the doorway of a little shack chatting to a lady in the boiling hot sunshine. Actually, she was chatting to me and I was just listening, as my Portuguese consisted of only a few basic phrases and words. My two most important phrases were '*Meu nome é Cally*' and '*Onde é o banheiro?*' ('My name is Cally' and 'Where is the bathroom?').

These two phrases were very important to me as I can live for several hours or even days without eating, but not without going to the bathroom!

So, as I listened that day, I smiled and nodded my head in an attempt to show that I understood some of what she was saying. However, it was a really hot day, and I began to feel decidedly uncomfortable. I could feel my scalp, where my long hair was parted, beginning to prickle with the heat. I began to chide myself for not taking my hat with me that afternoon. I said to God, *Father, please help me, I really need a hat*. It wasn't exactly intended to be a 'prayer'. Just one of those moments when we cry out to our Father, like a child asking their daddy for something they need.

The woman looked over my shoulder at the sound of an engine. Moments later, a car appeared, moving slowly along the dirt road. It was a strange sight as the passengers were throwing pieces of paper out of the windows. I wondered what was happening, until I remembered that it was soon to be election time in Brazil. These were members of a political party, distributing information to persuade people how to vote.

What a waste of time and money, I thought to myself. *Most of these people have nothing or little to eat, and here are the politicians throwing them pieces of paper. They need food, medicines and education. Anyway – most of them are illiterate, and won't even be able to read the leaflet. And... Lord, if only I had brought a hat!*

In the next moment I had one of the most amazing experiences in my whole life. The car drew closer, and the people around me were grabbing at the pieces of paper floating to the ground. Children were running alongside the car, and people were jeering and shouting and laughing.

There was an air of commotion as the car drove past me, and without warning a hat flew out of the back passenger window and landed on my head. It was a red cap with the number of the political party printed on the front. How incredible that at exactly the right moment it landed on my head.

I laughed out aloud, and put my hands to my head in delight. The people around me laughed with me, sharing my joy. However, they had no idea of the significance of that moment. I was unable to explain just *how* amazing it was. They didn't realise I had just prayed and asked God to send me a hat.

Later that day, as the sun set, and I no longer needed my miraculous hat, a man in the *favela* asked me for it and I gave it to him. I was so full of gratitude for the way God had met me so powerfully there in that slum – just when I needed Him most.

Chapter Twelve: Miracle Vehicle

There are two ways to live your life. One is as though nothing is a miracle. The other is as though everything is a miracle.
Albert Einstein[21]

After my first visit to São Paulo in 1998 I realised that I would need a car. The city is huge, and I knew my work would require me to travel long distances every day. Some good friends from Milton Keynes understood my need, as they had lived and worked in São Paulo for ten years. They also knew the dangers of a young, blonde foreigner travelling alone on public transport.

These friends have supported me financially since my work began with 'Signpost for Schools' in 1994. A few weeks before leaving for São Paulo in 1999, they phoned and invited me for coffee. It was so good to talk to them, as they knew São Paulo well, and had lots of good advice. As I was about to leave, they gave me an envelope with a cheque inside.

'This is for you to buy a car in São Paulo,' they said. 'There should be enough to pay for the car and the insurance for the first year.'

[21] Alice Calaprice, *The Ultimate Quotable Einstein* (Princeton, NJ: Princeton University Press, 2011).

I was overwhelmed by their generosity. Cars are very expensive in Brazil, and I had no idea how I was going to be able to buy one. That was the first miracle.

Now with the money in my hand, I had a huge challenge ahead of me. What type of car should I buy and where should I buy it? How would I know if I was being charged the right price, or if the owner would exploit me for being a foreigner?

When I arrived in São Paulo I prayed, and asked God to lead me very clearly to the right car dealer. I also prayed for wisdom to know which car to purchase – one that would be reliable and useful for my work. I had seen a car called a 'Towner' made by a South Korean firm called Asia Motors. Towners are mini people-carriers with seven seats, and this seemed like the ideal car for me. I would be able to transport children and adults from the *favelas* and streets, and not worry about having enough seats.

Father, I think a Towner is what I need, I prayed. *But, Lord, I need to know exactly the right one.* I decided to be extremely specific. *Please give me a turquoise Towner, with the letters of my name on the number plate. Then I will know very clearly that I should buy that car!*

That was my very specific prayer. My maiden name is Cornes, and so I knew that if I found a Towner with the letters C, O, R , N, E or S, then that would be a sign for me to buy it. I had also seen turquoise Towners, and that is one of my favourite colours.

'This is so exciting,' I told my Brazilian friend who had offered to help me choose the car. We were on the way to a car dealer in São Paulo; one that she knew was trustworthy. 'I can't believe that today I might be buying my car. Mind you, I'm not sure how I'm going to learn to drive in São Paulo. The traffic is crazy, and I've only ever driven on the other side of the road in England.'

'Yes, it'll take a while to get used to,' she laughed. 'If you ever do.'

My driving experience in Brazil would certainly be very different from driving in Milton Keynes. The roads there are designed in a grid system, with horizontal and vertical roads linked by roundabouts. Even in the rush hour the traffic flows quite easily.

São Paulo couldn't be more different, and in rush hour no one rushes anywhere! The roads become gridlocked, and it can take hours to arrive at your destination. The council has tried to alleviate the situation by introducing the 'rodizio' or 'rotation' system. This means drivers are restricted from using their car during the morning and evening rush hours, on a certain day of the week. This restriction is determined by the final number on their number plate. The idea is to reduce the number of cars on the roads at those specific times. It works to a point, but most people just buy two cars with different numbers at the end of their number plates.

'Here we are,' my friend announced, driving through the gate of the car dealer. There was a large courtyard area and I could see various cars for sale. She parked the car, and my heart began to race with excitement.

Would my car be here waiting for me? Would I find a turquoise Towner with letters from my name on the number plate? I realised we would probably have to visit several car dealers to find the right one, but to my surprise there in front of me was a turquoise Towner. I could feel my heart beating really fast. It was the only turquoise Towner in the car park. Two of my prayer requests had already been answered.

I looked anxiously at the number plate to see if the letters were the same as my name. I gasped. The turquoise Towner had the number plate COR 9418. That was what I had asked for. In front of me was exactly the car I had prayed for.

I jumped out of my friend's car and ran towards it. As I drew closer I stopped and stared. I realised that the number plate was in fact

CQR 9418, so what I had thought was the letter 'O' was in fact a 'Q.' However, the tail of the 'Q' was blanked out, and so it looked like an 'O' instead.

'This is my car,' I exclaimed to my friend in delight. 'This is exactly what I prayed for. Please ask the salesman how much it costs.'

My friend walked off happily in the direction of the office. This was going so smoothly. I stood looking at the car, overwhelmed by God's faithfulness.

What a blessing, I thought to myself. *God, You are awesome. You pay attention to even the small details of my life. I'm so grateful. Now, please, Lord, let it be the right price.*

I had R$13.000,00, which was the amount I had after converting my friends' offering into Brazilian reais. My friend appeared a few moments later with the salesman.

'The car is R$13.500,00, Cally,' she explained, 'but the man said he'll give you a discount as you're paying in cash. He will sell it to you for R$12.000,00.'

That's amazing, I thought to myself. *That will leave me enough to pay the insurance too.* My thoughts were interrupted as she continued, 'He said it's an excellent car. It has just one previous owner, and has only 9,000 kilometres on the clock. It's practically brand new.'

I looked at my car. The turquoise blue paintwork was gleaming in the sunshine, and I opened the driver's door to look inside. It was in really good condition, and the upholstery looked like new. The previous owner had obviously looked after it very carefully.

It took about half an hour to organise the paperwork, and we arranged to collect it the following week, as soon as I had arranged the insurance cover.

'Wow, that was quick,' my friend said, as we drove out of the car park. 'That was the easiest car purchase I've ever done.'

'Yes,' I replied. 'God took us to exactly the right place for me to find my car. He is so faithful.'

I settled back in my seat to enjoy the ride home. I began to dream of driving my new car around São Paulo. I imagined the children from the *favela* bouncing up and down in the seats. Most children who live in *favelas* don't have the opportunity to travel in cars. I knew my car was going to be a blessing in so many different ways.

Years later I looked at a photograph of my car, long after I had sold it. I realised that God didn't only confirm through the letters on the number plate, but through the numbers as well. The first pair of numbers, 94, was the year God called me to Brazil, in 1994. The next pair, 18, was the date I arrived in Brazil in 1999 on 18 January. God is awesome. I love it that when I pray and ask Him for specific details, He answers, and confirms His faithfulness in miraculous ways.

I have experienced God's protection upon my life and work many times. One morning I arrived in the *favela* and parked my car outside the church building where I was to work that day. I taught several English lessons to the children and adults and also visited a couple of the families. At the end of the afternoon I prepared to drive out of the *favela*. Two cars had parked in a rather haphazard way, in front of and behind my car, almost hemming me in. However, I was still able to manoeuver my small car out of the space with little difficulty. I drove home, tired but fulfilled after a good day's work.

The next morning I returned, and was met by one of my students, Amanda. She ran up to me, breathless, and obviously desperate to tell me something,

'*Tia, Tia* – you'll never guess what happened yesterday. Look, *Tia*. Look at the bullet holes!'

As I turned my head to where she was pointing, my knees began to feel like jelly. I looked at the two cars that had been parked either side of mine, and both were riddled with at least thirty bullet holes each.

'It's OK, Amanda, stay calm,' I said, taking a few deep breaths myself. 'What happened?'

'Just after you left yesterday there was a gunfight,' she explained. 'It was the drug traffickers, and they started shooting at each other. Then others joined in. That's why there are so many bullet holes in the cars. I'm sure they waited for you to leave,' she continued. 'It happened just two minutes after you left.'

I don't know if they waited for me to leave. Missionaries are highly respected in the *favelas* in São Paulo. Even the criminals and drug traffickers protect you rather than harm you. They know you are there to help them and their families, and they have an almost superstitious fear of hurting Christians.

If they didn't specifically wait for me to leave that day, then God's timing was perfect. If I had left just two minutes later, I would have been in the firing line. I realised once again how God had sovereignly protected my life, and gave thanks for another day to serve Him.

I never felt afraid working there, or in any of the *favelas* in São Paulo that I have visited. That first year working in the *favela* was the best possible training ground to prepare me for ministry in Brazil. I frequently go into *favelas* to visit families, and feel no fear at all. I just always have a deep understanding that I'm meant to be there, and that God will protect me.

In fact, in many ways I realise I have been able to do things and go to places that many Brazilians can't. One of the leaders from the *favela* church once said to me, 'Cally, you know, you have an anointing on your life and work here that we Brazilians don't have'.

'How do you mean?' I asked.

'What I mean is that you go into the homes of the drug traffickers, the murderers, the thieves, the drug addicts, and you go in the name of Jesus. So, because everyone knows you as the English lady with the blonde hair who looks after the children, they know you're here to help them. That means you're welcome wherever you go.'

I realised how privileged I am in being called to this nation, and given such open access to people's lives. I also made a decision when I arrived that I would love Brazil and not criticise or judge the people or the culture.

I heard a story[22] of a young man whom God called to serve Him in a country where it rained almost all the time. A native of the country said to him, 'I can't believe it's raining again. How do you put up with it?'

'I love the rain,' the young man answered.

'You love the rain?' the person replied. 'Are you crazy?'

'No, I made a decision to love this nation. God called me here, so I've chosen to love the rain, to love the people, to love the food, to love everything.'

That story made a huge impact on my life, and I made a decision to love Brazil. If you look closely at my eyes you will see that they are predominantly blue, but with flecks of green and yellow. Even my eyes are the colours of the Brazilian flag, and after twenty-one years in this country I feel more Brazilian than British in many ways. Twenty-one years ago I could never have imagined the adventures and challenges I would face as I fell more and more in love with this incredible nation, and its people.

---

[22] Source unknown.

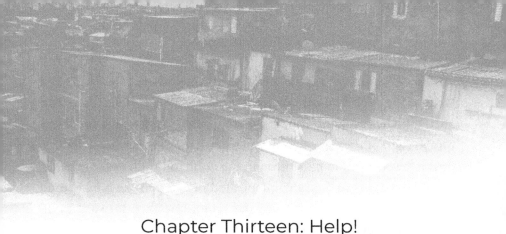

Chapter Thirteen: Help!

Enter his gates with thanksgiving and his courts with praise;
give thanks to him and praise his name.
(Psalm 100:4)

A few weeks after my arrival in São Paulo I began to pray earnestly for God to help me learn Portuguese. I had always enjoyed languages at school, and considered a university degree in Linguistics if my dancing career didn't work out.

My knowledge of French and Latin certainly came in handy for learning Portuguese, as there are many words that are similar or with the same root. The problem was the high speed at which people spoke, as it just sounded like gobbledygook.

I felt like a dog wearing a muzzle. I so desperately wanted to communicate, but all I could say were a few words and phrases. Even when I asked them to speak more slowly I still didn't have sufficient vocabulary to understand what they were saying.

I became more and more frustrated, and so one day I asked God to give me a supernatural understanding of the words that people said to me. I also asked Him to help me understand and remember words that I had maybe heard once, but not memorised.

A few hours later I left the missionary hostel where I was living and went to the bank to draw out some cash for the first time. There was an automatic revolving door at the front of the bank, and a small box on the right of the door for customers to deposit their metal objects. This allowed them to pass through the door and walk into the bank.

I waited my turn, and then deposited my keys in the box. I stood back behind the yellow line on the ground, walked forward to go through the revolving door, and it stopped.

Oh, that's strange, I thought to myself. *I must have something else that is metal in my bag.*

I delved deep into my handbag and found a metal pen. I deposited that confidently, and tried again. That didn't work either. I went back behind the line, reached into my pocket, and found some coins. I deposited them in the box but once again the door stopped. I noticed there was now a long queue of people along the pavement outside the bank. A few were grunting with impatience, obviously not happy with me, this incompetent foreigner who was making them wait.

The guard inside the bank, who had noticed my dilemma, began to shout at me through the glass door. I couldn't hear very well because he was on the inside and I was on the outside. He was shouting the same word over and over again. It sounded strange, something like, 'Wah, wah, wuva, wah, wah, wuva.'

Oh Lord, please help me, I cried in my head. *I have no idea what a 'wah, wah, wuva' is.*

I started to perspire, sweat dripping from the back of my neck and trickling down my back. I could feel my face growing redder and redder. I wondered if maybe I should just run away, and pretend I didn't need to go into the bank anymore.

I suddenly remembered my prayer of that morning, asking God for supernatural understanding. The queue grew longer, the grunting grew louder, and my prayer became more and more desperate. The guard shouted louder than before,

'Wah, wah, wuva, wah, wah, wuva.'

God, please help me, I shouted inside my head. Suddenly from nowhere I remembered the word *'guarda-chuva'*. I looked down to see my small umbrella lodged in the side pocket of my handbag. I pulled it out triumphantly, and deposited it in the box. I skipped swiftly behind the yellow line to prepare for my entrance. Now scarlet in the face, feeling like a drowned cat, I stepped across the line, and the door began to revolve!

The guard clapped his hands in glee, the grunters in the queue sighed loudly with relief, and I gave thanks to God!

Thank You, God. My faithful, gracious God. Thank You so much for helping me understand. Once again God heard my prayers and rescued me.

Chapter Fourteen: My Cup

If you believe in prayer at all, expect God to hear you.
If you do not expect, you will not have. God will not hear you
unless you believe He will hear you; but if you believe He will,
He will be as good as your faith.
Charles Spurgeon[23]

My work in the *favela* during my first year in São Paulo was excellent preparation for what was to come. I had begun to understand the Brazilian culture, and had learned to speak and understand Portuguese. I had also gained the confidence I needed to walk into potentially very dangerous places and situations.

During that first year I also began to pray for my '*cup*'. I had been alone for eight years after my first marriage ended, and I longed for a husband, and the '*cup*' for my saucer. I prayed I would find a man of God who would share my same heart for the poor. I asked God for a man who would be willing to serve Him, whatever the cost, and wherever He sent us.

One day I prayed a desperate prayer.

---

[23] *The Church of England Magazine* (London: Edwards and Hughes, 1848).

God, please hear me! How long must I wait? I so want to meet my husband, the man of God you're preparing for me. I don't know if I can wait much longer. I know I have to be patient, but my patience is running out. Please, Lord, send me my husband!

The following week I was at the missionary hostel where I lived, getting ready to go to the *favela*. It was quite early in the morning and I walked out of my bedroom, rubbing my eyes and contemplating the day ahead. I was taken by surprise to see a very good-looking young man sitting quietly on the sofa. He looked up and saw me.

'Hi there,' he said, in Portuguese. 'Do you remember me?'

Flustered by his question and searching for an answer, I blurted out, 'No!'

'Well, I remember you,' he said calmly. 'We met in the *favela* last year. Do you remember now?'

I did indeed remember. This was George, a young Brazilian man who I had met on my last day, during my first visit to São Paulo in 1998. He was a friend of the pastor who led the organisation I was working with, a British man who had worked in São Paulo for many years. The pastor had invited George to go to the *favela* on my last day, to help film the children and the project. They were making a fund-raising video for the Baptist Missionary Society (BMS), and George had offered to help.

Wow, he's a bit nice, I thought to myself, and sat down to chat. I tried to apologise for my forgetfulness.

'Sorry,' I said. 'I do remember you now. What are you doing here today?'

He explained, speaking slowly and clearly, that he was going to help with another video for the BMS harvest appeal. The film crew was staying at the missionary hostel, and I had been asked to go along too. I was even more pleased to have been invited now. Who was this young, good-looking Brazilian man? I felt interested in finding out more.

The next few days were a whirlwind. George and I spent all our free time getting to know each other, a spark of interest igniting quickly into a flame. However, our attempts at conversation were difficult. George didn't speak English and I only spoke basic Portuguese. We spent a lot of time looking for words in the dictionary, but it didn't seem to really matter that we couldn't communicate.

We both felt something so strong between us and were obviously enjoying each other's company. We talked about our lives but it was difficult to understand everything he said, and a few things about his past confused me. But my heart fluttered like a million butterflies every time we met, and I sensed something was blossoming between us.

However, I knew if this relationship was to continue, then I would have to tell him of my divorce.

He's single and is from a strong Christian family, I thought. *Will he want me when he knows?*

For all these years after my divorce I had felt like second-hand goods. I doubted that anyone would ever want to marry me. My self-esteem was so low after the break-up of my first marriage. I prayed really hard about George, and if it was right for us to take this friendship further.

I didn't want this to end. I couldn't face him rejecting me, but I knew I had to tell him. It wouldn't be fair to lead him on, so I summoned up the courage and picked up the phone. My hands were shaking so much I could hardly press the buttons. I felt like my heart was in my throat. George answered the phone and I blurted out in my pigeon Portuguese, 'George, I need to tell you something.'

'No, you don't,' he replied. 'I already know.'

I thought he hadn't understood what I had said, so I tried again. This time my heart seemed to be sitting on the top of my tongue. I wondered if it would drop out of my mouth and I would die, right there and then. I could hardly say the words. 'George, I need to tell you something. It's something really important.'

Once again he replied, 'No, you don't. I already know.'

I was so confused. Didn't he understand what I was saying? I didn't know any other way of saying it in Portuguese.

'Well, what do you know?' I asked.

His answer came like a thunderbolt, almost knocking me to my knees.

'I know you're divorced. I've known that all along. When I met you that day last year, I wondered who you were and wanted to know your story. I asked Diana and she told me everything, including that you're divorced.'

There was a long silence. I opened my mouth to reply, but no words would come out. A huge sense of relief overwhelmed me like a wave and I began to cry. There was more silence, and then George asked, 'Why are you crying?'

'I thought you wouldn't want me,' I managed to blurt out.

'Of course I want you. Your divorce isn't important to me. It also doesn't matter that you're seven years older than me. What matters is what we feel for each other. The past is in the past.'

We talked for a few more minutes and arranged to meet later that day. I hung up the phone and fell to my knees, thanking God and wondering what He had in store for us.

Was George really my 'blue and yellow cup'? Was this the man God had chosen for me? Was this true love for us both?

The next few weeks were like a hurricane. My feelings and emotions were whipped into a frenzy of love and hope. At the same time I felt insecurity and doubt. Was this true love at last? Could I trust him? I prayed and asked God, *Lord, I don't want to be hurt again. Can I trust George?*

'No, you can't,' I sensed God reply. 'But you can trust Me.'

Several friends warned me that it might not be right, that we should wait and not rush into it. My mind was a whirl of confusion. I had no appetite for food and hardly ate a thing for three weeks. We met every day and spoke of our hopes for the future together. We both wanted to be married, and realised we were falling in love.

However, there was a big problem. I had to leave Brazil. My six-month tourist visa was due to expire a few weeks later and I had to return to England. I prayed hard and asked God for help. I didn't want to leave Brazil and I didn't want to leave George. I knew God had called me there and I longed to start working with the street kids. They were the real reason I had gone in the first place. I also longed to marry George, and begin our ministry together.

George took me to the Federal Police station in the centre of São Paulo. There I learned that I could leave Brazil, cross a border, and renew my visa for another ninety days. That would give us long enough to organise the wedding in the civil registry office. As a result, I would have residency status and would be able to get married.

Now I had to make plans. Which border should I cross? How, when and with whom? A few days later a friend who I had met at Bible college contacted me and asked if she could visit. She was curious to meet this strange, dark Brazilian man whom I intended to marry, and so she made arrangements to visit São Paulo.

We planned a visit to the Foz do Iguaçu waterfalls. They are situated on the borders between Brazil, Argentina and Paraguay. This was perfect! The plan was in place. We would travel there together, see the waterfalls, renew my visa and George and I would be able to get married. I wasn't aware that it would be quite so complicated.

'Do you realise your tourist visa runs out in two weeks' time?' the huge Federal policeman at São Paulo airport asked. He was more than six feet tall, and towered over me menacingly.'You'll have to leave Brazil, and return to England. Then you can't return until next year.'

'Oh, yes, I know,' I replied confidently. 'I went to the Federal Police office in the centre of São Paulo. They told me there that I can cross a border, and renew my visa for ninety days. I am on my way to Foz do Iguaçu now to do just that.'

I felt so relieved knowing that it would be straightforward and simple. Just a stamp on my passport, and my future was sealed.

'Sorry, madam, but that regulation no longer exists. Even if you cross a border, the most you will be given is fourteen days.'

I couldn't believe what I was hearing. Surely he was wrong. Tears welled up in my eyes, and I didn't understand how two policemen from the same police force could have such different information. I asked again, hoping I had misunderstood.

'But the policeman in São Paulo, he told me what to do. I have to go to the border, and get a stamp on my passport. Then I will have ninety more days in Brazil.'

He beckoned to his colleague, another enormous police officer, and called out to him.

'She wants to stay another ninety days. Can she renew her visa on one of the borders?'

'No, she can't,' the man shouted back. 'The rules have changed. Just fourteen days.'

The first policeman turned to me, and repeated himself, speaking slowly as if I were an alien.

'Madam, the rules… have changed. You have to leave… in fourteen days.'

He shoved my passport back into my hand, and I burst into floods of tears. We continued through customs, and the tears rolled down my cheeks uncontrollably. My friend tried to comfort me for the next few hours but I was inconsolable.

How could it all have gone so wrong? How was I going to stay in Brazil to work with the street children? How was I going to marry George? Would I have to go home and miss my wedding? Would I ever be able to return to Brazil?

We arrived at our little hotel and I phoned George. I cried all over again as I tried to explain what had happened. He reassured me he would get everyone he knew to pray, and a little spark of hope returned to my soul.

Could there be any chance the policeman at the airport was wrong? Could God do a miracle and give me ninety more days instead of fourteen? My mind reeled with questions and doubts, and I could hardly sleep that night, wondering what was in store for me at the border crossing.

The next day we set off to see the vast and majestic Foz do Iguaçu waterfalls. The views were breathtaking, and the sound of the water falling onto the river below was almost deafening to our ears. Rainbows danced on the surface of the water, the spray of the falls glistening in our hair. It was one of the most exhilarating experiences of my life.

It would have been even more wonderful if I hadn't had so many doubts in my mind. The next day I needed to find the border.

Where should I go? What did I have to do? How many days did I have left in my beloved Brazil?

'Excuse me, but do you know how I can renew my visa, please? I have to go to one of the borders.'

A kind tour guide called Luigi was sitting opposite me in the van. He had agreed to take us to see the falls earlier that day, and I wondered if he would be able to help me.

'Of course. It's easy,' he replied. 'You just go to the border with Paraguay. I can take you tomorrow if you like.'

My heart skipped a beat.

Tomorrow? Tomorrow I would know how many days I had left? I wasn't sure I was ready but I knew I had to face this. I had to trust that whatever the outcome, God was in control.

The next day we met Luigi at the bus stop. He took us into Paraguay to the border town of Ciudad del Este. We went off in search for the town centre of this bustling and colourful market town. A few hours later, armed with fake perfume, earrings and bracelets, we set off to the border to sort out my visa.

First we arrived at a little kiosk where a Paraguayan border guard gave me a ticket.

'Cross the bridge, and take this to the office on the other side,' he barked. I didn't understand what he said and had to ask him to repeat himself. I realised he was speaking '*Portanhol*', an unofficial mixture of Portuguese and Spanish, which was why I barely understood.

We walked quickly and purposefully across the bridge, every step taking me closer to the truth.

Would I be leaving in just fourteen days? I didn't even want to contemplate the thought. I walked into the office, and went straight up to the counter. There was a glass window between me and the giant-sized border guard. His neck was almost as wide as his shoulders, and his biceps were bulging beneath his short-sleeved uniform. His cheeks were so large his eyes seemed to be buried inside them. He peered at me through the glass.

'Yes? Can I help you?'

Perspiration was pouring down my face. My pulse was beating so loudly in my throat I was certain the guard could hear it. My mind went blank. I couldn't remember any of the words I had rehearsed to say. What I was doing in Brazil, why I wanted to stay... Nothing came to my mind, and I blurted out in my worst Portugese ever, 'I want to stay another ninety days in Brazil, please!'

The guard grunted, and motioned for me to hand him my passport. I pushed it under the glass and he examined it closely. He flicked slowly through every page, and then looked even more slowly at every page again. It felt like I was standing there for at least an hour. I felt like sweat was now flowing from every pore of my body.

He scribbled a number, thumped my passport hard with his stamp and thrust it back under the glass window. I grabbed it and fumbled, trying to find the right page. Eventually I found it and looked at the number. My whole body shaking, I peered at the scribble and had no idea what it said. It didn't look like 14 but it also didn't look like 90. Was it 20, 60 or no, surely not, just 10?

'Excuse me, sir, what does it say?' I asked, feeling like the ground was shaking beneath me.

'Ninety days,' the guard bellowed, and I leapt into the air, dancing and waving my passport around wildly. My friend hugged me, and laughed as she saw my delight.

Thank You, Lord. Thank You, Lord. You answered my prayers. Oh, why did I doubt You? I knew You could do it!

The return journey to São Paulo was quite different from our journey to Foz do Iguaçu three days earlier. My mind now was full of street kids and *favelas*, wedding dresses and pageboys, hopes and dreams, prayers and thankfulness. Now I could stay in Brazil forever. Now I had my '*cup*' for my saucer. We would be together in sickness, health, poverty and wealth (well, probably not very much financial wealth), till death parted us.

I could never have imagined in a million years what lay ahead. I could never have dreamt of the challenges, joys and heartaches in store for me.

Chapter Fifteen: Blankets and French Fries

Be faithful in small things because it is in them that
your strength lies.
Mother Teresa[24]

Our wedding day was perfect. The marriage ceremony was in a large
Baptist church in the centre of São Paulo. The pastors from the *favela*
church where I had been working hired two buses, and packed them
full of all my friends from the *favela*. When I walked into the church
and down the long aisle, I saw their smiling faces looking at me. They
were all sitting in the front rows of the church, the place reserved for
the most important guests!

Honeymoon over, we returned to São Paulo and I was longing
to start work on the streets. It was now the year 2000, and almost
every day I remembered that call that I had felt six years before, in
my bedroom in Milton Keynes. Sometimes it seemed like another
lifetime, but now I had a yearning within me to actually begin the
work I had gone there to do.

---

[24] https://www.goalcast.com/2017/04/10/top-20-most-inspiring-mother-teresa-quotes/ (accessed 2.1.20).

It wasn't, however, that simple, as George and I both needed training. We asked God to help us find an organisation, and people who would teach us to work with street kids. Around that time a card arrived through the post. It was from a girl I had met during one of my trips to India.[25] She wrote to me about a Brazilian man she knew, who had contacts with YWAM in São Paulo. She had felt she should contact me, and sent me his number.

I called him, and told him of our desire to work with street kids. He was very helpful, and put me in contact with a Brazilian couple who were working with the street children with YWAM. I was overjoyed, as at last I would be able to actually work on the streets with the children who live there, not just in the *favelas*. I phoned them and the following day we met up to talk about joining their team.

The following Monday I woke up and literally jumped out of bed. It was the first day we would be working with the street kids. I had no idea what to expect. I forced myself to eat, despite my lack of appetite. I knew I would be hungry by the end of the day, and wanted to be ready for action.

I felt a strange mixture of excitement, apprehension and joy. I'd been waiting for this day for such a long time. At last I would be able to meet some of the thousands of children I had read about who make the streets their home in São Paulo.

We drove to the centre of town and our friends were waiting for us at the arranged meeting point. We prayed together, and set off to find the children. These people had been working on the streets for several months and knew where to find them.

We stopped in front of a bank where about twelve children of varying ages were sitting on the ground. They had positioned their mattresses in front of the bank, and their blankets and clothes were

---

[25] I went on three mission trips to India between 1992 and 1997.

strewn all over the pavement. There were broken flip-flops, empty bags of glue and plastic carrier bags full of clothes. The youngest looked about six years old, and the eldest about twelve. I discovered that day that street kids are severely undernourished, and in fact the youngest was ten, and the eldest eighteen. They were dressed in old, ragged clothes and most were barefoot.

They jumped up to greet us, and a huge lump appeared in my throat. I struggled to hold back the tears and didn't really know what to think or feel as a mixture of emotions welled up inside me. I felt grateful that at last I was able to meet children similar to those I had read about all those years before. I also felt so sad to see these precious children living on the street, and hoped that I would be able to do something to help them.

I was shocked by their appearance. They were dirty and thin, their hair a tangled mess and full of head lice. They invited us to sit with them on their old mattresses that lined the pavement, and I sat down next to two girls who were sisters. One was thirteen and the other was eleven. I noticed the soles of their feet were filthy from walking barefoot. Their faces were also dirty. Really dirty.

We chatted and laughed, and I felt so happy to be there with them. They called me '*Tia*' and tried to speak to me in English, so I taught them some new words. I asked them how children like them end up living on the streets.

'Most of the street kids have families, *Tia*. Most have a mum or a grandma living at home. Sometimes they have a dad but not often, and usually each kid is from a different dad. Our mum has ten kids including us, and is pregnant again,' one of the girls answered. 'Our mum doesn't work so she sent us out to beg at the traffic lights. Every night we would go home late after begging all day, and our mum would spend the money on alcohol.'

'We went to bed hungry most of the time. If we spent some of the money on food, she would beat us so badly we could hardly walk the next day,' the older girl added.

'We started sleeping on the street instead of going home, and the older kids living on the street looked after us. When our mum's last boyfriend moved in, we weren't welcome at home anymore. She doesn't seem to notice we're not there anyway,' the younger girl said sadly.

I felt an overwhelming sense of disbelief that any mother could allow her children to live on the streets. I remembered my mum and the way she cared for my every need, always by my side and pouring out her love. Images of her sitting in the car waiting for me at my dance lessons flashed through my mind.

The older girl interrupted my thoughts.

'It's better on the streets, *Tia*. We can buy food with the money we get from begging. We have friends to hang out with, and I have a boyfriend. We're going to have a baby,' she said smiling, 'I'm five months pregnant already.' She pulled up her T-shirt to reveal her stomach. She didn't look pregnant at all, and I imagined her baby wasn't developing properly.

I tried to conceal my shock. This thin, undernourished, thirteen-year-old girl was pregnant. I felt I should pretend to be happy, but just wanted to cry. She was just a child and she was the one needing to be cared for. Now she had a life inside her that would be born on the streets. What chance did that child have for a different future?

'Oh,' I replied, searching for words to say. No words came out of my mouth but verses from Psalm 139 flashed through my mind:

For you created my inmost being;
you knit me together in my mother's womb.
I praise you because I am fearfully and wonderfully made;
your works are wonderful,

I know that full well.
My frame was not hidden from you
when I was made in the secret place,
when I was woven together in the depths of the earth.
Your eyes saw my unformed body;
all the days ordained for me were written in your book
before one of them came to be.[26]

'Did you know the Bible says God knows us right from when we were in our mother's womb?' I asked. The girl looked at me surprised, and shook her head.

'God knows your baby too, and is knitting him or her together right now.'

She smiled up at me, and as I looked at her I realised that the dirt on her face was in fact glue. It was black, and was stuck to her nose and all around her mouth.

'Almost every child who lives on the streets in São Paulo sniffs glue,' my friend from YWAM explained to me later. 'It takes away the feeling of cold and hunger and helps them forget why they're living on the streets. "Sniffing glue", however, actually isn't "sniffing" at all, as they inhale it through their mouths. That's why the glue gets stuck to their faces, and they find it really hard to wash it off.'

I took a wet wipe out of my bag and gently began to clean the girl's face, teasing off the glue without hurting her skin. She closed her eyes and I could tell she was enjoying the attention.

'God loves you so much, and He's here with you all the time,' I told her. 'You can dream of a different future for you and for your baby. You shouldn't have to live on this street. If you want to, you can leave

---

[26] Psalm 139:13-16.

and we'll help you. But please don't keep sniffing glue. Everything you put inside you goes into your baby. What you eat, what you drink, what you smoke and the glue you sniff, it's all going into your baby and will affect the way he or she grows and develops.'

She looked at me and nodded. I knew she would continue sniffing glue, but I wanted to at least try to warn her. I later discovered that most children born to street-girls have learning difficulties and respiratory problems because of the glue their mothers sniffed during the pregnancy.

The smell of stale urine pervaded the air, and I realised that this was their toilet too, especially at night when no public toilets were open. I tried to imagine being pregnant and living on a street. 'Here you are,' a passer-by said, and thrust a box of McDonald's fries into one of the girls' hands. I didn't know what to think. I was pleased someone had helped. At the same time, I wondered if fast food was their main diet. I was aware of how bad that would be for their health, and especially for that unborn baby. I wasn't prepared for what was to happen next.

'*Tia*, here you are, do you want some? You must be hungry,' the younger girl asked, placing the box of fries in my hand. 'And, here, pull my blanket over you, you must be feeling cold.'

Once again tears welled up in my eyes, and I swallowed hard several times. I didn't want to cry in front of the girls.

Wasn't I supposed to be there to help them? I thought I had gone there to show them God's love. And now they were looking after me.

'No, thank you, they're for you. Please, you eat them,' I insisted.

'No, *Tia*, we want you to have them,' the older girl replied.

'No, you eat them,' I insisted again. The box of fries was passed back and forth between us, and we burst out laughing,

'Let's share them, then,' the younger girl suggested. We all tucked into the warm fries, huddling together under their blankets as the cold wind whipped past our faces.

I felt like I was right in the centre of the hand of God. I had a real sense of peace that I was where I was meant to be, right at that moment, in the centre of His will. I remembered the children on the Mumbai station platforms. I remembered the tears I cried that night as I promised to serve God wherever He sent me.

A few hours later, I drenched my pillow with my tears once again. This time, I wept for the street children of São Paulo. I wondered which one I would rescue, and prayed there would be many more than just one.

Chapter Sixteen: Hell of a Hideout

This job has been given to me to do. Therefore, it is a gift. Therefore, it is a privilege. Therefore, it is an offering I may make to God. Therefore, it is to be done gladly, if it is done for Him. Here, not somewhere else, I may learn God's way. In this job, not in some other, God looks for faithfulness.

Elisabeth Elliot[27]

One of the challenges of working with street kids in São Paulo is to know where to find them. They don't always hang out on the streets, but live in '*mocós*', inside bridges or deserted buildings. *Mocó* is the name given to any place where the children hide out from the police, or others who might wish them harm.

One afternoon I went to visit a group of street children who were living in a *mocó*. My friend from Milton Keynes was visiting, and I wanted him to meet all the different people I was helping.

A *mocó* is one of those places that have to be seen to be believed. This particular dwelling place was inside a bridge over a main road, and the access was through a heavy iron gate. The only reason I knew it was there was because one of the street children had shown me.

---

[27] Elisabeth Elliot, *A Path Through Suffering* (Grand Rapids, MI: Revell, 2003).

If not, I wouldn't have known it even existed. It felt like going into hell on earth every time I visited that place.

The entrance was always ankle-deep in water, sometimes quite clean if one of the girls was washing clothes, but more often than not with a strong smell of urine. There was no bathroom, and so this part of the entrance area was used as their toilet.

As usual we clapped our hands outside the gate, the Brazilian equivalent of ringing the doorbell. Andrea, one of the girls who lived there, appeared out of the darkness and opened the gate for us. She was in her early twenties and had lived on the streets most of her life. Her face was thin, and she had dark rings under her eyes. She hugged me first and then hugged my friend.

'Come in, *Tia*, don't look at the mess,' she joked.

We walked through to their 'living area' and my eyes slowly adjusted from the bright afternoon sunlight to the dim light inside. It was a large room with several curtain-like hangings made of old sheets. These 'curtains' separated those who wanted to use drugs or have sex from the general living area. The light came from bare bulbs, with various wires precariously strewn across the walls and ceiling.

There was an old sofa, and several filthy mattresses on the floor. There were a few makeshift shelves made out of wooden fruit boxes in the kitchen area; also a very dangerous-looking improvised stove, hooked up to a gas canister. An old kitchen cupboard was propped up against one of the walls, with the doors hanging off. The battered old television was switched on, with a children's programme blaring at full volume. I was impressed that even in a place like this the young people had made it their 'home'.

There were several children playing with an old plastic cup on the floor, and two were sitting half-asleep on the sofa.

'That's Felipe,' Andrea pointed to a little boy. 'He's two, and he had an accident last week. His mum was cooking noodles and the pan of boiling water spilled on his arm.' I looked at the little boy, and could see his forearm was covered with a filthy bandage. I shuddered at the thought of this horrible accident, and his burnt skin underneath.

Two small babies were asleep on the mattresses.

How can a baby or child survive in a place like this? I thought.

'How are you doing, Andrea?' I asked.

'I'm good, *Tia*, just the same as normal.'

'Do you ever go out, Andrea? You don't stay here all the time, do you?'

'Most of the time, yes, *Tia*,' she replied. 'Most of us are too scared to go out because of the police. Some of the kids are on the run from prison, so they can't ever go out.'

One by one the children greeted us with a hug and a kiss, and Andrea motioned for us to sit down on the sofa. I strained to be able to see in the darkness, and felt a little nauseous with the mixture of smells. Urine and weed, coffee and stale vomit. I tried not to breathe too deeply, feeling so sad that a place like that even existed.

I concentrated on chatting to Andrea, and asked her about the little boy and his burns.

'Is he going to be alright? It must have been a nasty burn,' I said.

'Yes, he had to go to the hospital, but he's better now,' Andrea replied. 'Accidents like that happen all the time here.'

Her nonchalant response didn't surprise me at all. Tragically, it isn't unusual to see a child on the streets with severe burns, which happen from accidents like this, or worse. Some children are even burnt as they sleep on the streets. A street-girl may be 'owned' by a boy for sex, and no one else is allowed access to that girl. If a boy talks to or even just looks at a girl who 'belongs' to another boy, then he will suffer the consequences. One common punishment is that while he sleeps the other boy will find him, douse him in petrol, and then set him on fire. Many children die this way or are permanently injured with severe burns.

Andrea stood up to put hot water in a pan, and I remembered the day a few months earlier when I was sitting on the streets and playing with a young boy. His name was Davi, and he was nine years old. He was unable to walk properly as his legs were so badly burnt. He moved around by sitting on the ground and swivelling his bottom and feet from side to side, in a crab-like action. The skin behind his knees was so tight from the burns, he wasn't able to stand and stretch his legs properly.

After a few minutes of colouring pictures and chatting, he laid his head on my lap, and began to fall asleep. Stroking his hair I asked, 'Didn't you sleep well last night, Davi?'

'*Tia*, I never sleep at night,' he replied. 'I'm too scared they will burn me again. They threw petrol on me, and set fire to me. I can't get to sleep at night anymore.'

I swallowed hard, and took a deep, long breath. I couldn't believe what I was hearing.

Why did someone do that? I thought to myself. *What could this thin, undernourished little boy have done to deserve such a punishment?*

I remembered Mumbai, and my nose pressed against the train window. The images of children clinging to each other as they slept on the platform raced through my mind. Did God show me that to prepare me for this moment?

I hugged little Davi as he fell asleep on my lap. My heart broke for him, and for many others like him, burnt, maimed and murdered in senseless attacks. I cried into my pillow that night, long and hard. Mumbai tears that now became São Paulo tears.

Before leaving for Brazil I had prayed many times for God to soften my heart for those who were broken. Now I felt like my heart was breaking for these children. I remembered the people over the years who had said to me, 'Oh, I couldn't do that. I couldn't go to a *favela*, to the streets, or into the prisons. It would upset me too much. I wouldn't be able to cope.'

My reply is always the same.

'No, you probably won't be able to cope, but ask God to give you the strength. Allow God to break your heart. Go where He sends you, and then allow yourself to weep. Weep into your pillow at night. Drench your pillow with your tears. Then dry your tears, and go and do something to help. Doing nothing is not an option.'

My thoughts were interrupted as suddenly a girl called Noela burst into the *mocó*. She had lived on the streets for many years, and was a lively girl with a tendency to speak her mind. She rushed in, and threw herself down on the sofa.

'Hi, Noela, are you OK?' I asked. There was obviously something very wrong as she looked around her nervously, and refused to answer. I then realised that she had been followed into the *mocó* by three adults – two burly looking men, and a woman. They all stomped in, and stood in the middle of the room, right in front of me, glaring at Noela.

The atmosphere in the room was very tense as everyone looked in the direction of these three menacing figures. They all appeared to be extremely angry. The men had surly faces, with broad shoulders and bulging biceps. The woman, however, was the one that most concerned me. She had an expression on her face of pure hatred, her lips twisted downwards, and her eyes like little slits as she stared at Noela.

I realised that something was very wrong. My heart was racing. Andrea had quickly returned to my side so I leaned over and whispered into her ear, 'What should I do? Is it best for me to go, or stay?'

'*Tia*, get out of here, *now!*' she whispered back.

I could feel my heart beating in my throat as I stood up. I looked at the men, giving them direct eye contact, shook their hands firmly, and said in the best Portuguese I could muster, 'My name is Cally, I'm a missionary, and I'm leaving right now. Goodbye.'

They seemed to be taken aback, as they hadn't noticed me sitting there, and one of the men replied politely, 'Oh, yes, lady, of course, nice to meet you.'

At this moment, my friend also stood up. The two men glared at him, and before they could say anything I said, 'And this is my friend, he's also a missionary, and he's also leaving.'

The two men shook his hand, and we left the room.

As we reached the open air and the sunlight hit us full in the face, my knees nearly buckled beneath me. I was shaking. The perspiration dripped from my forehead, and ran down my face. I licked the corner of my mouth, and tasted the salty sweat about to drip down my chin.

'Oh my goodness, I've no idea what's going on,' I blurted out in a half-whisper.

'What should we do? my friend asked.

'I don't know,' I replied, straining to hear what was happening inside. 'I think we should stay here for a few minutes. If we hear shouts or screams we'll have to go back in. Let's pray.'

We prayed for peace and for no one to be hurt, and after a while we made our way home. During the journey I was trying to work out why those three strange people had appeared in the *mocó*. I kept asking myself if we should have stayed, and if we could have done anything to help.

I know Andrea would have asked me to stay if they needed me. She seemed so sure we should leave. Maybe I did make the right decision. Or maybe we should have stayed? I was really confused and concerned.

That night, Isabela, one of the girls from the *mocó*, phoned, and told me what had happened. Noela had been walking along the street quite near the *mocó*. She stopped and asked the woman with the very angry face for a cigarette. When the woman refused, Noela began to swear at her and complain loudly. The two men, one of whom was the woman's husband, decided to follow Noela and beat her up a bit, just to teach her a lesson.

'*Tia*,' Isabela exclaimed, 'those two men were from the PCC!'

My heart skipped a beat. The PCC stands for the '*Primeiro Comando do Capital*' (the 'First Command of the Capital'.) They're a mafia-type gang who rule the city of São Paulo in the prisons, the streets, the businesses etc. They're a highly organised group and even have their own lawyers. They're not to be messed with, and can be extremely dangerous people.

I asked Isabela if Noela was hurt, and she said no. She was sure the men knew we would stay nearby to listen, and so they just gave her a telling-off instead of a beating.

Later that evening my friend and I were chatting in the kitchen, and we realised what a potentially dangerous situation we had faced that afternoon. I was aware of the faithfulness of God and how once again He had protected us from harm.

Chapter Seventeen:
Dignity, Hope and a Future

If you find it in your heart to care for somebody else,
you will have succeeded.
Maya Angelou[28]

'Try the doorbell just one more time,' I suggested.

'There's no one in,' George replied. 'They would have answered the door by now.'

'Please, let's just try one more time,' I insisted.

We were standing outside the apartment belonging to Vitoria's mother, Sandra. This was our first 'family visit' after beginning our work with the street kids. Vitoria's story was similar to many of the street children.

At the age of six, her mother took her and her brother and sisters to live on the streets. They had no money to pay the rent and were struggling to eat. On the streets they were able to beg for money and didn't have to pay bills. Sandra and Vitoria's brother and sisters had now moved into this very poor apartment building, but Vitoria had run back to the streets.

---

[28] Ann Kannings, *Maya Angelou: Her Words* (Morrisville, NC: Lulu Press Inc, 2014).

Our friend from the project where we were working as volunteers had met her living on the streets, and encouraged her to go to live in a children's home. Vitoria was now ten years old and she liked the idea of staying in a real home far from the streets.

'Cally, George, please could you visit Vitoria's mother?' our friend asked. 'I'm concerned that she doesn't know where Vitoria is, and I'm sure she will be relieved to know she's safe and well cared for. Here is her address. Please tell her where Vitoria is living, and that she can visit whenever she wishes.'

The apartment door was on a landing with various other similar doors. There was no lift and the stairwell we had just climbed was filthy, with graffiti scrawled all over the walls. There was a stench of urine and damp, and the sound of loud TVs coming from all different directions.

Children ran up and down the stairs, some racing past us at high speed, others more slowly, carrying baby brothers and sisters with some difficulty. I stared at the shabby front door and wondered where Sandra, Vitoria's mother, might be.

'It's no good,' George said. 'We'll have to come back another day.'

I was frustrated. This was our first opportunity to visit a street kid's family, and I didn't want to go home yet. I wanted to be the bearer of good news and tell Vitoria's mother that her daughter was safe and well.

We were just beginning the long descent when a young woman appeared. She was extremely thin, and out of breath from climbing the stairs. She had a plastic carrier bag in her hand and walked past us to the same front door where we'd been waiting.

'*Dona* Sandra?' George asked. (Women in Brazil are often called 'Dona' before their name as a mark of respect.)

'Yes,' she replied, a little suspiciously.

'Please, don't be alarmed,' George replied. 'We're from a project that helps street kids, and we've come to tell you that Vitoria's safe and well.'

Sandra breathed a deep sigh of relief, and held up the carrier bag in her hand. She opened it, and motioned for us to look inside. It was full of documents, photographs and papers.

'I've been searching for her for days,' she said. 'No one could tell me where she was. She does this all the time. Just disappears and I have to go looking for her.'

Sandra opened the front door. 'Please come in and sit down,' she said, gesturing for us to go into the living room. The room had just an old torn sofa and one wooden chair. There was a piece of material hanging haphazardly as a makeshift curtain above the window. Although the room was almost bare, it was clean, and was obviously home to Sandra and her family.

'Vitoria's in Juquitiba,' George began. 'She was found living on the streets in the centre of São Paulo.'

'I can't understand why she always runs away,' Sandra complained. 'She knows the dangers, and yet she always behaves like this.' Her words came out slowly and falteringly. She spoke with a stutter, and hesitated in between every few words before speaking again. 'I'm not well.' She stopped again, but this time it seemed she was struggling to choose the right words to say. 'I have "*the* disease", you know?' She looked at us, and we nodded, acknowledging that we understood. 'You know, the one that has no cure? My husband got it in prison, and passed it on to me when he came out.'

I felt so sad for *Dona* Sandra as I knew she was referring to HIV.

'I have the herpes virus too,' she said, and lifted her T-shirt at the side to show a large strip of pus-filled spots along her ribcage. I could see every rib poking through her skin, her trousers almost falling down from her emaciated waist.

'We're here to help you, *Dona* Sandra,' George explained. 'Vitoria's being well cared for in a children's home. You can visit her when you wish, and we'll drive you there as its a very long way from here.'

Sandra looked relieved, and her face broke into a grateful smile.

'Now *you* need to be cared for and we're here to help,' George said. 'We have a food parcel in the boot of the car. Would that be a good start?'

'Oh yes, please,' Sandra replied, obviously relieved. 'I have no job at the moment, and I need food for my son and two daughters.'

'We'll go and fetch the food parcel, but first, may we pray with you?' I asked.

'Yes please,' she replied. 'I'm Catholic. Is that alright?'

'Of course,' I answered. 'Your God's the same God as ours!'

We held hands in the centre of the lounge and prayed, asking God for healing, peace and provision. When we finished praying Sandra whispered, 'My neighbour downstairs, *Dona* Glória, she has the same disease. Could you pray for her too?'

'Of course,' I replied, wondering how many other people in this tower block would be so open to receiving prayer.

'I'll take you downstairs to meet her,' she offered, and led us out of the front door. She walked slowly and painfully down the stairs, and we reached the ground floor. She knocked at the door of the apartment.

'Come in,' a frail voice answered.

Sandra opened the door, and I saw the thinnest woman I have ever seen. *Dona* Glória was sitting on the sofa, and looked as though the smallest gust of wind would blow her away.

'These are my friends, Glória,' Sandra explained. 'They're looking after Vitoria in a children's home in Juquitiba. They just prayed for me, and I said I was sure you would like prayer too.'

'Of course,' Glória exclaimed, her voice stronger now, obviously encouraged by our visit. 'And maybe you could take this boy to that home too,' she said, pointing to the other side of the room.

I turned my head, and saw a small, thin boy of about eight years old kneeling in the corner, facing the wall. I noticed there were kernels of corn scattered on the floor around him, and realised he was kneeling on top of some of them. His shoulders shook up and down as he cried silently.

'He's a real problem,' Glória explained. 'I don't know what to do with him. My teenage daughter is giving me trouble too. I have to put a chain around her neck, and chain her to the bed to stop her running to the streets.'

I was shocked at *Dona* Gloria's words.

'Stand up, Israel,' she barked, and the little boy stood up. He shook the corn kernels off his knees, and came over to greet me. I held him gently by the hand, and he sat willingly on my knee. He looked at me and smiled with big tears running down his cheeks.

'Hi, my name's *Tia* Cally,' I said. 'We came to visit *Dona* Sandra, and help her family. We can help you and your family too, OK?'

Israel nodded, and wiped away the tears with the sleeve of his very dirty T-shirt.

'Let's pray, shall we?' I suggested. Everyone stood up, and held hands in a circle. I grasped Israel's hand and squeezed it tightly, looking down into his eyes as he stood staring up at me. We all closed our eyes and I took a deep breath. I didn't quite know where to begin.

I prayed for healing and for peace in that home. I prayed for God to bless *Dona* Glória with good health, and with wisdom to raise her many children. I prayed for God's provision and for unity in the family.

George and I delivered the food parcels to the two families and then said goodbye. We returned to our car, and as soon as the door was shut I burst into floods of tears. George took my hand and squeezed it.

'Did you see the corn, George?' I cried. 'Israel was kneeling on corn. That's so cruel.'

'That's normal here,' he replied. 'It really hurts, and the parents know it.'

Two weeks later we returned to visit *Dona* Sandra. We climbed the flights of stairs, this time with more hope that we would find her at home. We arrived at her door, out of breath, our brows wet with perspiration. I knocked on the door and we waited a few moments. Sandra had been waiting for us, and greeted us with a huge smile.

'Guess what?' she asked excitedly. 'I've put on two kilos since your last visit, and my herpes is almost gone.' She lifted her T-shirt, and the pus-filled spots were now a faint red rash across her ribs. Even the bones seemed to be protruding less than before. I gave her a big hug, smiling to myself as I am always trying to 'lose' weight, not put it on! However, I understood that for *Dona* Sandra this was a huge victory, and it was so good to see her looking stronger.

I've accompanied Vitoria and her family ever since. We led weekly Bible studies with various families in that apartment block, and saw many answers to prayer. Vitoria stayed at the children's home for seven years, and today is married to Clayton, a pastor and professional builder. They have a baby son called Nathanael, who is like a grandson to me, and it is such a joy to see how God has restored Vitoria's life. She struggled in her teens when she returned home for a period, and we took her to a women's rehabilitation centre where she stayed for four years. This helped her in many different ways, and although she and her husband struggle financially, she is firm in her faith and love for God.

Before her marriage to Clayton, she and all her family members lived in one of the poorest *favelas* I have ever visited. A few years ago, she sent me an urgent message saying that a fight had broken out in the *favela*. A couple who were neighbours of Vitoria and her sister, had started to argue and the husband threw the gas canister at his wife. She dodged but it exploded and their shack was set on fire.

At least fifty of the neighbouring shacks were completely destroyed, including those where Vitoria and her sister's family were living. They were able to salvage only a few belongings and lost everything else – their clothes, furniture and electric domestic appliances. I contacted a church in the area and asked if they could help. They rallied round and donated everything that the families needed. Vitoria's sister, Marissa, received the donations, and was able to help Vitoria and twenty-four other families with the donations she was given.

A few years ago, I received a message from Vitoria.

'Cally, guess what? Clayton asked me to marry him. We're getting engaged.'

This was wonderful news as Vitoria is like a daughter to me, and we began to pray about how to help them. I mentioned the news in a prayer letter, and several people sent donations. George and I offered to pay for them to get engaged at the same restaurant where we were engaged in 1999. It is a very special restaurant on the forty-second floor of one of the tallest buildings in São Paulo. A friend paid for our meal when we got engaged, and we were so blessed by the experience. The view from the restaurant is breathtaking and it's such a romantic place to get engaged.

We really wanted to give them the experience of a lifetime. There is a tendency for people to give 'poor' things to the poor. We give our old clothes and shoes, our used kitchen equipment and toys. We wanted to do the opposite and give Clayton and Victoria the best experience possible.

So, a few months later, they were engaged at the 'Terraço Itália' restaurant, on the forty-second floor. We bought their rings, new clothes and paid for their meal. They told us afterwards that they didn't even recognise most of the items on the menu, but they said it didn't matter. They had the night of their lives and we were so excited to bless them in that way.

We also continued helping *Dona* Glória and her family for several years. We took her daughter to the same children's home as Vitoria. She was tired of being chained to the bed and admitted she needed some help. She stayed for a few weeks, received the help she needed and then returned home. She never ran away to the streets again, and is now married with a family.

Israel always held a very special place in my heart, and when he was seventeen I met him again. I was leaving the youth prison after leading a session there, when I heard a voice behind me: '*Tia* Cally? *Tia* Cally?'

I turned and saw a young man, his hands handcuffed behind his back, with a guard by his side. He stopped and said, '*Tia* Cally, do you remember me? Israel? *Dona* Glória's son?'

I ran towards him, and hugged him tightly. The guard was taken aback with surprise.

'Sorry,' I explained hurriedly. 'I knew Israel years ago. I haven't seen him for a long while.'

The guard loosened his grasp. 'How long have you been here?' I asked.

'A few months.'

'Which unit are you in?'

'Belém.'

'Fantastic,' I exclaimed. 'That's where we work. I'll ask if you can take part in our group!'

'Oh, that would be amazing, *Tia* Cally,' Israel replied, his face beaming and his eyes shining.

'Don't worry, I'll sort it out. See you soon,' I said, and hugged him again.

A few weeks later Israel joined our group, and we accompanied him for a few years after his release. Sadly, he went back into crime and has been in the adult prison for several years. He is due to be released, and I intend to contact him and help him find work.

That is one of the greatest challenges when the boys are released, as they find it so difficult to find employment. Most of our boys are black, from poor families and live on the outskirts of the city. They have a mindset that tells them they have just two choices. The first choice is to work in a car wash. It is low risk, but poorly paid and has no status. The second is to be a drug trafficker. This is high risk, extremely well-paid, and high status. It isn't difficult to understand why they choose the latter.

Our goal is to help them dream of a different future, where they can study and find a good job. One of my many dreams is to set up a company that employs ex-prisoners and gives them the opportunity to work and provide for their families.

One of the challenges of helping the poor is to find ways of enabling them to help themselves. If we keep giving them a 'fish' they will depend on us forever. We need to give them 'the fishing rod' and help them learn to use it. That gives them dignity, hope and a future.

Cally – 3 years old   Cally – ballerina 1982

Cally – performing 'Mad about the boy' Adeline Genee Theatre 1983

Cally – professional actress
1985

Cally – Baptism 1991

Cally and Ben 2001

Cally's car – Chapter 12

Cally and Joe

Igor and Cally

Anita and Antonio's house

Anita and Antonio

Cally and Laisa

Cally and kids

Thiago receiving a cesta
básica (food parcel)

São Paulo

Street-kids

Old lady in favela –
Chapter 26

Families living inside bridge

Favela 2017

Boy on top of rubbish cart

Cally being honoured as High Ambassador of the
Brazilian Academy of Literature, Arts and Culture 2018

Psychodrama group 2019

Psychodrama scene 2019

Cally, Ben and Joe 2019

Chapter Eighteen: The Warehouse

Love intentionally, extravagantly, unconditionally.
The broken world waits in darkness for the light that is you.
L.R. Knost[29]

I had been working with the street kids for a few months when I met Lidia and Livia – two sisters with big brown eyes, long dark-brown hair and slim prepubescent bodies, skimpily dressed. Lidia was twelve and Livia was ten when I first met them. Their mum, Pamela, had ten children, nine girls and a baby boy, each child from a different father.

'Let me take you to see your mum,' I suggested. 'This street shouldn't be your home. You're in such danger here, especially at night, sleeping on the streets. Please let me help you.'

'No, *Tia*,' Lidia replied. 'We don't want to go home. Our mum doesn't want us, and we don't want to live there. She has a new boyfriend. He's our baby brother's dad. We can't go home if he's living there.'

---

[29] https://www.goodreads.com/quotes/9106284-do-not-be-dismayed-by-the-brokenness-of-the-world (accessed 7.2.20).

My heart broke to hear her words. She seemed adamant, but I still couldn't believe that her home could be worse than the streets.

'How about if we just go and visit?' I suggested. 'Maybe things are better at home now, and your mum will have you back?'

The girls looked at each other and shrugged. 'Alright, *Tia*,' Livia replied. 'We'll go and visit, but we're not staying, OK?'

'OK,' I replied. 'Let's go.'

We walked along the streets, arm in arm, laughing at the pigeons pecking each other.

'We've never been in a car, *Tia*,' Lidia said. 'This is going to be an adventure.'

I tried to hide my surprise that children of their age had never travelled in a car. I realised it made sense. Their mother was so poor she certainly wouldn't have a car, and they'd lived most of their lives on the streets.

'Oh, I tell a lie,' she exclaimed. 'I did go in a car once. It was a police car. Two cops took me to the police station when they caught me stealing. I didn't stay there long, but I had to walk all the way back here. I didn't mind too much as they put me in the boot of the police car on the way there, with handcuffs on, and I got bruises from the bumpy ride. Today's going to be much better.'

'It certainly is,' I said. 'Now let me help you with your seatbelts.' As soon as they were ready, we set off. They giggled wildly every time I went over a speed bump, and played with the buttons that lowered and raised the electric windows.

After about half an hour we arrived at their home. It was in a dingy back street in a very poor area of São Paulo. It didn't look like a house, as it was just a hole in a long, high wall.

'Follow us, *Tia*. I'll call my mum,' Livia said. I walked behind them through the hole in the wall, into a huge deserted place. It was so dark it took a few moments for my eyes to focus. Some of their sisters saw them arrive and ran to greet them. I looked around me and couldn't believe what I was seeing.

This wasn't a home. It was a warehouse, and everywhere I walked there were piles of human excrement. Some of their little sisters were sitting on the ground, crying or moaning. They were filthy, and their hair was matted. Their faces were crusted with dirt, the snot from their noses running into their mouths. The girls led me to the corner of the warehouse, behind a partition, where there was a double bed and a few old mattresses strewn on the floor. That was the bedroom area and it was obvious there were no bathroom facilities.

'What are you doing here?' a woman shouted, appearing from behind the flimsy cardboard partition. I realised this was their mother and she was totally drunk, swaying from side to side and slurring her words. Her hair was a mess, her eyes were bloodshot and I wondered how she had got into this state.

'I told you not to come home, you know I've got too many ****** kids to look after,' she ranted.

Obviously embarrassed, the girls half-hid behind me, and Livia said quietly, 'Mum, this is *Tia* Cally, she's come to help us.'

'I told them not to come home,' she continued shouting, now looking in my direction. 'All they do is misbehave, and I've got too much to worry about to look after them as well.'

'Is there any way I can help, *Dona* Pamela? Could I get you a food parcel?'

'That would be very helpful, yes,' Pamela replied, more calmly. 'My husband's unemployed and I lost my job too.' I looked over her shoulder and saw a young man sprawled on the bed, a little baby boy crying helplessly by his side, the man ignoring his cries.

I went to buy the food, some nappies and some snacks, and I just wanted to cry. I realised why the girls were so adamant about not going home. I took the food parcel out of the boot of the car, and returned to find Pamela asleep on the bed, snoring loudly. One of the older girls, a child of about eight, was feeding the baby with a bottle of milk.

'Tell your mum I'll come back tomorrow,' I told the children, handing some cookies and juice to each one. I drove the girls back to the streets, wondering what I could do to help.

'Lidia, Livia, you're right, it can't be easy to live in your home. Your mum needs help and so does your whole family. However, it's still too dangerous for you to live here on the streets. I know of a children's home out in the countryside. Would you like to go and live there? You can live in a real house, go to school, sleep in your own bed, eat good food, play and swim. What do you think?'

'I'd like that,' said Livia. 'I don't like living on the streets. What about you, Lidia?'

'Mm, I don't know,' Lidia replied. 'I need to stay with Lina.'

'Who's Lina?' I asked.

'Our older sister,' she answered. 'She's thirteen, and she's the one that took us to the streets. I don't want to leave her by herself. I think Livia should go. She gets really scared at night and can't sleep.'

'Can I talk to your mum about it tomorrow, Livia?' I asked.

'Yes, *Tia*, and I hope she says "yes".'

The next day I picked Livia up from the streets, and we visited Pamela again. It was earlier than the day before and she was more sober. She agreed to Livia going to the children's home, and we packed a few clothes into a carrier bag.

'Bye, Mum,' Livia said. 'Come and visit me, OK?'

'I'll try,' she replied.

Livia kissed her baby brother and her little sisters goodbye, and turned and left. I took her to the same home as Vitoria, and she lived there for several years. I loved to visit her and see her dressed in clean clothes, her hair in ringlets and a big smile on her face. She was so happy there and was doing really well at school. Her mother moved to a *favela* a few months later, and we helped her for many years. On various occasions we took her to visit Livia, and she was happy her daughter was being cared for. Livia left the home when she was about fifteen, and I heard she now has her own family.

George and I welcomed several street children into our home over the years, on a short-term basis, when there was an emergency or their lives were in danger. Emilene came to stay for a few nights when her older brother was threatening to kill her. She was from a large family, six boys and three girls. The three sisters lived on the streets, and the six brothers lived at home. They were incredibly poor and we helped them with food parcels and other basic necessities. On the day Emilene came to stay, I cooked dinner and placed the food on the table.

'Let's give thanks,' I said.

'*Tia*, let me pray, please,' Emilene interrupted.

'Of course,' I replied. 'Thank you.'

A few minutes later we began our meal.

'Emilene, that was certainly a long and thankful prayer,' I said.

'Yes, *Tia*. I'm extremely grateful for this food. I've been eating just fat and flour for the last three days.'

'Fat and flour!' I exclaimed. 'What do you mean?'

'I go to the butcher and ask for scraps at the end of the day. It's mostly the fat they've cut off the meat, and I take it home, melt it in the frying pan and mix it with flour. That's what we eat at home almost all the time. When the market is open I go there just as they're closing down and sweeping the road. I pick up the rotten vegetables on the ground and make them into soup. That's how we survive, *Tia.*'

I am a different person since that day. I thank God for my food and His provision on a daily basis with a very thankful heart. I once heard a pastor talking about people who thank God for the food in the shopping trolley while in the supermarket queue. It saves them from having to thank God at every mealtime.

I want to thank God for all that He provides for me. I choose to thank Him for every meal and every provision. Emilene was just a young girl who lived on the streets, but she taught me many things. She is thirty-one now and has two sons, and she's like a daughter to me.

When you help people who have nothing, then you realise you have everything.

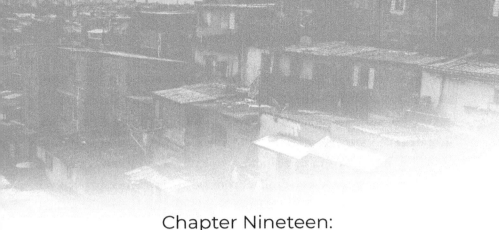

Chapter Nineteen:
Fleas and French Perfume

Faith is the evidence of things unseen.
Maya Angelou[30]

Igor was not a typical street-dweller. He spoke six languages: Portuguese, English, Spanish, Italian, French and German. He had worked most of his life in the Brazilian Air Force, and was a highly intelligent and articulate man. Sadly, his addiction to alcohol meant he had lost everything, including his family and his home.

He wore the same old pair of trousers every day, held up at the waist with a piece of string. His hair was long and tangled and his moustache was always embellished with crumbs of food. His matted beard was long and hung down on his chest, full of rice and fluff and an infestation of fleas.

Igor was always very happy to talk to me in English. We chatted about the Queen and politics, fish and chips, and The Beatles. He told me stories of the countries he had visited and his adventures in the airforce. If I arrived on the streets in the early afternoon, he was lucid and the conversation was easy to follow. However, if I arrived in the late

---

[30] Maya Angelou, *Rainbow in the Cloud*. See also Hebrews 11:1.

afternoon then conversation was almost impossible. He was almost always drunk and half-conscious, lying sprawled on the pavement.

One hot sunny afternoon I arrived to find Igor lying on his back in a drunken state. I knelt down to speak to him and he began to convulse, his arms and legs shaking violently. His mouth contorted and his teeth clenched as he rolled from side to side uncontrollably. I quickly grabbed an old blanket from beside him and carefully placed it under his head. I stayed by his side, praying and waiting for the convulsion to pass.

None of the other street-dwellers seemed to take much notice. No one, in fact, was really aware of what was happening. The traffic continued to race past us, the street sellers continued to shout, and passers-by continued on their way.

I had been kneeling beside him for several minutes when I felt a tap on my back, then two more, one on my head and the other on my shoulder.

What's going on? I thought, and looked up to see what was happening. Igor was lying beneath a huge old tree, and its branches were full of pigeons. It seemed they were using me as target practice, bombarding me with their droppings. I couldn't believe it. I was in such a tense situation with Igor continuing to roll and shake and the pigeons were dropping their 'bombs' on me. I didn't know whether to laugh or cry.

After what seemed like an eternity Igor came round, and was confused and disorientated. I comforted him, and he became calm and fell asleep. I stayed with him for a few more minutes and then went to sit on a low wall nearby to get my breath and stretch my legs. A young woman in her twenties was sitting beside me, and we began to chat. She was dressed in a smart skirt and blouse, and her hair was tied back in a ponytail.

'I saw you helping that man,' she said. 'Do you work here with the street-dwellers?'

'Yes,' I replied, 'mostly with the street kids, but I've known Igor for a few months now.'

I noticed that he had woken up and was sitting against the wall. He was picking food out of his beard and mumbling to himself. I was relieved that he seemed to be back to normal.

'Why do you do what you do?' the girl asked.

'Well, I'm a missionary,' I answered. 'I really believe God called me to come here and work with the street kids and help the poor. I'm from England, by the way. How about you? Do you have a faith?'

'Kind of,' she replied. 'I was raised a Catholic, but I don't go to mass anymore.'

It was a beautiful summer evening, and the sun was beginning to set. Children were playing hopscotch on the pavement beside me and a baby was crying. Two women passed by me, chattering excitedly, and car horns blared from the rush-hour traffic. As we continued talking I could tell something was wrong.

'I'm so sorry,' the young woman said. 'I don't think I can stay here much longer.'

'That's a shame,' I replied. 'Do you have somewhere to go?'

'No,' she answered, screwing up her nose. 'I'm really sorry. I don't want to be rude, but the smell of that man you were helping is so strong. I think I'm going to have to leave.'

Igor was indeed very smelly. He was probably the dirtiest, smelliest man I've ever met. It was obvious he didn't bathe or ever wash his clothes. I was used to working with the street kids and adults, and I think my sense of smell had become less sensitive. I didn't seem to notice that his smell was so strong anymore.

However, to someone not used to it, his smell was almost unbearable, and I could understand why the girl felt she had to leave. I looked around to see if there was somewhere else we could sit, but there were no more spaces further along the low wall. At this time of day the square was full of street-dwellers, students and traders.

Please, Lord, help me, I prayed. *I want her to know about You. I don't want her to leave just because of the smell.*

We continued chatting for a few more minutes. I breathed in deeply. A beautiful fragrance like French perfume filled my nostrils. The wind was soft on my face and I looked around to see where the fragrance was coming from. A stall was selling flowers a few feet away, and the gentle wind was wafting the fragrance in our direction.

The girl didn't leave, and we sat and talked for over half an hour. I told her my story of how I had met Jesus and then I prayed for her, that she would also know Jesus as her Lord and Saviour. As she stood up to leave, she noticed that Igor was still sitting nearby. I could tell she was confused that she could no longer smell him, and I pointed to the flower stall.

'See, Jesus loves you so much He sent a beautiful fragrant breeze to stop you leaving.'

Her mouth dropped open as she realised what had happened. She hugged me tightly and thanked me for our chat. I said goodbye and then looked for Igor who was no longer sitting under the tree. I found him across the square in a bar, drinking a glass of neat *cachaça* called Pinga, a traditional Brazilian spirit made from sugar cane, which is very cheap.

'Could I have some money for dinner, please?' he asked, slurring his words in otherwise perfect English.

'I'll buy you a meal,' I replied, not wanting him to spend my money on Pinga.

I ordered some rice, beans and meat, and he tucked into his meal. I said goodbye and made my way home, glad for my afternoon spent on the streets.

A few weeks later I arrived in the same place and looked for him, but he wasn't there.

'Have you seen Igor?' I asked one of the street-dwellers.

'He died,' he replied. 'Seems he ate some food from a rubbish bin and didn't realise it was mixed with rat poison. That's what they do to us, you know. Have to be careful what you eat.'

I felt so sad to hear this news and know I wouldn't see Igor on the streets again. It seems he died a painful, lonely death like many other street-dwellers, and I wished I could have helped him more.

Chapter Twenty: The Youth Prison

The purpose of life is to discover your gift. The work of life is to develop it. The meaning of life is to give your gift away.

David Viscott[31]

'Do you think we could stay and play a game of football with the boys, Cally?' one of the youth team asked. 'Please ask the director if we can. It would be so cool, Brazil versus England!'

It was the year 2000 and George and I were visiting a youth prison with a group of young people from England. Their presentation of sketches, songs and testimonies was lively and animated. Each item was received with a huge round of applause, and the boys joined in willingly when required.

I watched their faces, each one enthralled by the presentation. They listened with interest as the young people spoke in English and were translated into Portuguese. The presentation came to an end and I breathed a sigh of relief. I was glad it had gone so well, and grateful for this young team of enthusiastic volunteers. Now it was time to leave the courtyard area, but it seemed everyone wanted to stay a while longer.

---

[31] Kevin Cashman, *Leadership from the Inside Out: Becoming a Leader for Life* (Oakland, CA: Berrett-Koehler Publishers, 2017).

'Excuse me', I said to the director, who was standing by my side. 'The team are wondering if it would be possible to have a quick game of football with the boys. Would that be possible, please?'

'I don't see why not', he replied, and went and whispered to one of the guards who informed the boys they could play. They organised themselves quickly into a team, and removed their flip-flops, which they left in a tidy row by the wall.

I had dreamed of this day for a long time. Several of our street kids had been imprisoned over the past few months, and I was frustrated to lose them into the prison system. I was curious to know what the conditions were like, and how the young people were treated.

We'd arrived at the prison early in the morning, after a long journey in the rush-hour traffic. The first thing that struck me was the height of the walls towering above us. I hadn't really known what to expect, but the nine-metre-high walls seemed threatening and higher than I'd imagined.

After passing through the main gate, we then had to stop at various checkpoints. At each one we were body-searched by the staff, female guards for the girls and male for the boys. It was a simple search in which we raised our arms sideways at shoulder level, and they checked for metal objects, or items concealed in our pockets.

I discovered later that these searches were nothing compared to the rigorous body searches on visiting days for the boys' relatives. At that time, and still in some prisons today, visitors are required to remove all their clothing. This is to check that they are not concealing any weapons, drugs or mobile phones.

All visitors, men and women alike, then have to open their legs wide, and squat down three times, in front of a prison guard. The families are subjected to this humiliation and embarrassment on every visiting day, before they're allowed to enter the prison. Fortunately, body-scanning machines are now being installed in most prisons, and visitors no longer have to face this awful humiliation.

I only faced this experience once, during a visit to an adult male prison. George and I had been invited to sing at a wedding between one of the inmates and his fiancée. He had become a Christian at a church meeting in the prison, and the pastor suggested he should marry his partner. Men in prison in Brazil are allowed 'intimate visits' with their girlfriends, wives or partners on visitors' day. If they become Christians in prison, many of them choose to marry in order to do what they believe is the right thing before God. I will never forget the embarrassment of having to remove my clothes, and the female guard staring at my body as I performed my three squats. I couldn't imagine having to endure that every weekend.

Eventually we reached the prison unit, after filing through a series of gates and heavy metal doors. Each door clanged behind us with a loud bang, just to remind us we were well and truly locked in. The young volunteers were visibly nervous and a silence fell on the whole group. We had to wait a few minutes for the prison director to arrive, so we joined hands and prayed. I held hands with the two young people either side of me, and felt their clammy, sweaty palms. I could tell everyone was anxious so I prayed for peace, protection and for God to use us to show His light in that dark place.

Finally, the director arrived, and we entered the courtyard area to meet the boys. All eyes turned towards us as we filed in, smiling and trying to conceal our nerves. About sixty boys were waiting for us, most of who were seated on the dusty ground. A few were reading or chatting in groups, and others were leaning against the grey painted walls, talking or staring into space. Those closest to us instantly greeted us, questioning us enthusiastically about our visit.

After a short wait another member of staff arrived, and organised the boys, who had to sit in perfectly formed rows on the ground. The courtyard area was bare and dusty, and the sun was hot on everyone's heads.

The presentation was over and now the football game began. Any language barrier was overcome by the sheer joy of playing together. There was a competitive spirit, the boys from the youth prison trying their hardest to show that Brazil was better than England. They won, 3-1, but the team from England were delighted to have been able to play.

The director then explained that we were going to be taken to a side room and given refreshments. The staff had prepared plates full of food, and the team tucked in enthusiastically. There were '*pão de queijo*' (little pastry balls flavoured with cheese), mini croissants stuffed with frankfurter sausages, and cakes of various flavours. There was orange juice and '*Guaraná*', the typical Brazilian fizzy drink made with berries from the Amazon.

I had the opportunity to talk to the director of the unit, who expressed his gratitude for our visit. We talked for a few minutes about the youth prison.

'I was wondering if you could tell me,' I asked. 'What happens to the street boys after they're released?'

I wasn't prepared for the director's reply.

'They go back to the streets,' he answered.

Something inside me exploded at that moment and a silent cry, deep within me, shouted, 'NO!' The director explained that the youth prison had no means of finding accommodation for the street kids, and that they often had difficulty reconciling them with their families. It was inevitable, therefore, that they had no option but to return to the streets after their release.

I was shocked. I had hoped that some policy was in place to help find the boys some kind of accommodation. I had imagined that their time in the youth prison would provide them with opportunities, and an escape from the inevitable return to the streets.

That day I made a decision to devote myself not only to rescuing those who were already living on the streets, but also to helping those who had nowhere to go after finishing their prison sentences.

Chapter Twenty-one: I Can't Go On Like This

Great moves of God are usually preceded by
simple acts of obedience.
Steven Furtick[32]

Rosana and her father had been living on the streets for several weeks. I met them huddled together on a street corner, sheltering from the wind, in a place where many other street-dwellers were also living. Most of them were adult men, unemployed, alcoholics and drug users.

I looked at little Rosana, just five years old, with her pretty face and enchanting smile. Her big dark eyes looked up at me through her long, thick eyelashes. A deep sadness filled my heart to see her in a place like this, surrounded by drunken old men and piles of rubbish. There was a strong smell of urine and stale alcohol right where Rosana was sitting.

Beside her, the ground was strewn with rotting mattresses and mouldy blankets. There were empty polystyrene pots that once held food, and plastic carrier bags stuffed with clothes. There were no toys or dolls and no children of her age to play with.

---

[32] Steven Furtick, *Sun Stand Still: What Happens When You Dare to Ask God for the Impossible* (Colorado Springs, CO: Multnomah Books, 2010).

'Would you like me to get you something to eat, Rosana? Are you hungry?' I asked, pulling my jacket tighter around me. Winter in São Paulo can be chilly, especially for those who live on the streets.

'Oh, yes, please, *Tia*,' she replied. 'My daddy hasn't got any money for food today.'

'What do you like to eat?' I asked.

'Oh, *Tia*, I eat everything,' she answered.

I remembered myself at age five, fussy about eating most foods, and wondered how a five-year-old could possibly eat everything. I then realised that when you're starving you don't have the chance to be fussy. Rosana wasn't bothered what the food was, as she just wanted to eat.

I returned with two polystyrene boxes full of rice, beans, chicken and salad. I handed the food to Rosana and her father, and they tucked in gratefully. Rosana took each spoonful of food, looked at it gratefully, smiled, and popped it into her mouth with a grin. I felt happy I was able to help a little, but was so concerned for this small child living on the streets.

Her father seemed kind and attentive, but I knew he wouldn't stay by her side all the time. There must have been moments when he would go off begging or stealing, and leave her all alone. Then she would be so vulnerable to all the dangers of the streets, especially surrounded by so many drunken men.

'I was wondering if you could help us?' Rosana's father spluttered, spitting rice and beans as he spoke. 'I would like to take Rosana back to Rio de Janeiro. That's where we came from, and we need to go home. I need thirty reais to pay the bus fares. Please could you help us?'

Something about his words didn't seem right, and I wondered if he was telling the truth. It was the first time I'd ever met a father and daughter living on the streets, and a string of thoughts ran through my mind.

Where's her mum? Has he kidnapped her? Do they really come from Rio?

Stop it, I thought to myself. *Why do you have to be so suspicious? What if it is true, and they really need the money?*

George was also concerned, and asked various questions to try to clarify the situation. He then turned to me and whispered, 'Can we give them the thirty reais to get to Rio?'

What should we do? I thought. *I want to help but we hardly have any money left. We keep giving almost all that we have, and there's never anything left for us. We have so many bills to pay this month, so what are we supposed to do? Are we supposed to respond to everyone's need, and then not have enough for ourselves?*

This was our first year of marriage, and we were working together on the streets. It was so hard as there was so much need. I wanted to try to help everyone I met, but we just didn't have enough money.

'I don't think we should, George. We really don't have enough money this month for our own needs.'

'But they need to get back to Rio, Cally. Can't we help them with the bus tickets?'

'I'm sorry, George, I don't think we should help. We need money to pay our bills.'

The conversation went back and forth, and we couldn't come to an agreement. Eventually we decided not to give the money, apologised to Rosana and her father, and left. A chilly silence hung in the air as we drove home. George didn't speak, and neither did I. I was angry that he didn't understand. He was angry that we didn't help Rosana and her father.

How am I supposed to do this, God? You've called me to work with the poor. I just don't know if I can continue like this. Everyone we meet needs so much help. How do I choose which person to give to? How do I know when not to give?

We arrived home, and still in silence George parked the car. I walked slowly into the house. My heart was heavy and my head ached from trying to hold back the tears. I knew the only thing I could do was pray.

'I'm going to spend some time with God,' I told George. 'I can't go on like this for the rest of my life, so I'm going to pray until I know what to do.'

I turned and walked up the stairs, and went into the spare bedroom. There I could be alone with God for as long I needed. Or maybe for as long as He needed!

I grabbed a box of tissues, and fell to my knees. I stretched out my arms in front of me and lay flat on the floor, my nose pressed into the carpet. The tears began to flow and I cried from the pit of my stomach. My tears formed a wet patch on the carpet under my face, so I moved to a dry patch and cried some more.

God, I really need to hear You, and I really need to know Your will. You've called me to work with the poor. Please speak to me, Lord. Please help me to know what to do. When I'm asked to give, should I give? Even when that means I won't have enough for my own needs? This is so hard, God. If You've called me to this for the rest of my life, I need to hear your will. Teach me what to do, Lord. Please speak to me.

The tears kept flowing, and I kept on praying. An hour went by. I cried until my head nearly burst. I prayed and listened, trying to understand what God wanted to show me.

When two hours had passed I began to feel a sense of peace, and at the same time complete exhaustion. I felt as though I had no more tears to cry and no more words to pray. From nowhere a voice came into my head. It said simply, 'You give, and I will give back to you.'

Startled, I replied, 'God! Is that what You're saying? That I just have to give, and You'll give back to me?' The words began to sink into my understanding.

But, hold on, so that means You don't give me the money first? I give what I have, trusting that You'll give it back?

This was all I needed to hear. I knew from that moment that I could trust God to sustain me. I understood at last that I could give with a generous heart, knowing He would take care of me.

I stood up slowly, stretching my aching body, and stumbled into the bathroom. I washed my face, and as I raised my head to reach for the towel, I looked into the mirror. Oh, what a mess! The pattern of the carpet was imprinted into my forehead and my cheeks were bright red from lying down for so long. My nose was squashed into a strange shape from being pressed into the carpet, and my eyes were red and bulging from crying for two solid hours.

I didn't care. My face would soon return to normal, but I knew I would never be the same. I knew God had spoken to me, and I trusted Him to keep His word.

The phone rang, and I ran downstairs to answer it.

'Hi, Cally, how are you?' a friend from church asked.

'I'm fine,' I replied, uncertainly, not knowing how to reply. She was a good friend but I didn't feel able to share what had just happened.

'Will you and George be at home this evening?' she asked.

'Yes, we're home. Why?'

'Could we pay you both a visit? Just for a coffee and a chat?'

'Of course.'

'See you later, then. We'll arrive around 8 p.m.'

'Great, thanks. See you later!'

I put down the phone and went into the lounge. George was sitting watching TV, and I sat beside him on the sofa. He laughed at my squashed nose and bulging eyes, and I shared what I felt God had said to me about giving. He hugged me tight, and I think he was relieved. He is such a generous person that he found it really hard to say 'no'.

We had a wonderful evening with my friend and her husband. We shared all different stories, and laughed and prayed together. The time came for them to leave, and they stood up to go. Just as they left the house our friend turned to me and said, 'Oh, by the way, Cally, there's a little something for you both on the lounge table. It's just behind the photo frame.'

Bewildered, I thanked him, and waved goodbye as they drove off down the road. George and I joined hands and we walked back into the lounge. Picking up the photo frame I turned it around, and found an envelope tucked into the back. I had no idea of the surprise I was about to receive.

'What's this?' I said, calmly opening the envelope. I looked inside, and to my surprise there were three crisp, blue 100 real notes.

'Three hundred reais,' I exclaimed. 'George! They've given us three hundred reais.' I dropped onto the sofa and realised the significance. I had refused to give thirty reais that day to Rosana and her father. God then promised me that if I gave, He would give back to me. So, I could have given that thirty reais as God had already prepared a way to give it back, and ten times the amount. What a lesson I learned that day. What a glorious lesson of knowing that I can step out in faith, and trust that God will provide.

That experience helped me in so many ways, and I was able to trust God in a new way from that day onwards. A few weeks later I was called to use my faith once again, when a family from one of the *favelas* needed our help. Aria's husband, José, a drug trafficker, had been put in prison, and Aria and her children's lives were in danger. He owed money in the *favela* and the drug traffickers were threatening to kill Aria and the children. We agreed to help them move out of the *favela*, away from São Paulo, and return to their home town in the north of Brazil.

We went to our church meeting that night at a big Baptist church near the centre of São Paulo. The church had so many members it outgrew its building and was holding its meetings in a circus tent. The worship that evening was joyous and lively, and I was happy we would be meeting Aria and her children shortly afterwards.

First they would come to our house to sleep, and we would give them a snack before bedtime. Then we would take them to the bus station the next day to travel home. Their beds were made up and everything was ready. All I needed to do was to buy fresh bread rolls on the way home to prepare the snack.

During the meeting the time came for the collection. The velvet bag was passing along the rows of people so I quickly looked into my purse, and saw I had just one five real note.

Oh, I thought to myself, *I only have enough money to buy the bread rolls, not to make an offering.*

'Do you want to put some money into the collection?' George whispered into my ear.

'I do, yes, but we only have five reais, and I need it to buy bread for Aria and the children.'

'Do you want to give what we have?' George insisted.

'Yes, I do, but what about the bread?'

'If you want to give, then give what we have.'

Opening my purse again I took out my last five reais, and put it in the velvet bag as it passed in front of me. I didn't know how I was going to buy the bread, but I somehow felt peaceful that God would take care of it. I enjoyed the sermon and I sang the final song with my heart full of praise. The meeting ended and we said goodbye to our friends seated next to us.

One friend, Felipe, hugged us goodbye and then called George over to his side.

'George, I'm sorry, I meant to give you this a couple of weeks ago. Here's the money I owe you from the last barbecue.'

Felipe pressed a note into George's hand. My heart started beating faster as I waited to see the miracle God was doing.

'You give, and I will give back to you,' God had said to me that day, a few weeks before. Now what was He going to give back?

I needed five reais for the bread, and I'd given five reais to the collection. George opened his hand and there before me was a note, folded in two.

'Five reais,' I exclaimed. 'Five reais. Five reais,' I shouted in delight, and danced around the chairs. God had given me back exactly what I had given, and exactly at the moment I most needed it. I gave and He gave back to me, just as He promised He would.

We left the church a few moments later, and George stopped at the bakery. I walked in holding my five real note triumphantly in the air. I looked at the other customers also buying bread. It was just a normal Sunday evening for them, but not for me.

I have never felt so content to buy bread in my whole life. We told the story to Aria and the children when they arrived, and we all devoured our bread rolls with very grateful hearts. I wondered how many more times I would see God work miracles in my life. I couldn't have imagined the things He was going to do.

Chapter Twenty-two: Becoming a Mother

… the one the LORD loves rests between his shoulders.
(Deuteronomy 33:12)

After working on the streets for a while, George and I took part in a course at the YWAM base in Belo Horizonte.

'We need your advice, please,' George said to the director. 'We're working on the streets in São Paulo, and we really want to open a home for the children. We want to give them a place where they can live, go to school, and be normal kids.'

'Tell me about your team,' the director replied.

'It's just us at the moment, Cally and myself.'

The director paused. 'Then my advice is, don't open a home. It'll shut in six months if you have no one to help you. Also, if you're the ones out on the streets, and that's your gifting, then you need to keep working on the streets. You'll quickly become frustrated staying in a home. For now, just go to the streets, love the kids and help them get back to their families.'

This wasn't the answer we were expecting, but it seemed like good advice. We didn't have a team, and it would have been wrong to try to open a home at that time. We went back to São Paulo to work with the street kids, and with a surprise. I was pregnant! Our first child was growing in my womb, and we both were delighted at the thought of being parents.

When I became a Christian, I began to read the Bible. When reading the Old Testament, I came upon a wonderful verse in Deuteronomy 33:12:

> About Benjamin he said:
> 'Let the beloved of the LORD rest secure in him,
> for he shields him all day long,
> and the one the LORD loves rests between his shoulders.'

I especially liked that last verse, 'the one the LORD loves rests between his shoulders', and read it to George.

'If the baby's a boy, can we call him Benjamin?' I asked. 'I love that name.' He agreed, and we both wanted to give him George's name too, so when one of my scans showed it was a boy, we named him Benjamin George.

I enjoyed being pregnant especially as I could be 'fat' for the first time in my life, and not feel guilty. As a dancer I'd always struggled with being thin enough. My endeavour to become a professional dancer had made me paranoid about losing weight, and I ate as little as possible for several years. I slept in plastic trousers that made me sweat, hoping my thighs would shrink during the night. In fact, the trousers just made me dehydrated and gave me spotty legs. So, for the first time ever, during my pregnancy I felt my body was acceptable and I didn't need to be thin.

I was adamant I wanted to try for a normal birth. I was terrified of Caesareans and epidurals, and searched for a gynaecologist who would accept my wishes. The public health system in Brazil is precarious and a health plan is the best option. In São Paulo most births in the private sector are Caesareans, as they are considered more 'convenient'. Doctors in general aren't willing to wait for lengthy births, so Caesareans are quicker and also considered less risky for the mother and child. I managed to find a doctor who would allow me to have a normal birth and was relieved I wouldn't have to have a Caesarean.

My due date was 18 June, and that morning I woke up with contractions.

'George, I think Benjamin's on his way,' I exclaimed. 'Please phone Dr Silas, and tell him we're on our way to the hospital, and that I'm having contractions every ten minutes.'

Benjamin was born that afternoon. Dr Silas had been willing to allow me to try for a normal birth; however, there were complications when my waters broke.

'Cally, there's meconium in the amniotic fluid. Benjamin's heartbeat is irregular, and I think a C-section will be necessary,' Dr Silas explained.

'Oh, please, doctor, let me try for a normal birth,' I pleaded.

'I'm sorry,' he replied. 'You have to think of the baby. If he swallows the meconium he could have respiratory problems, or even die. You have to put Benjamin first. I'll give you twenty minutes to fully dilate, otherwise we will have to do a Caesarean.'

Twenty minutes later I was wheeled into the operating room, and shortly afterwards Benjamin was born by C-section. What a wonderful moment to hear my child's first cry, and be a mother at last. I was thirty-six years old, and had waited a long time for this moment.

However, the birth and the few hours afterwards were very different from anything I had imagined or hoped for. After a quick glance at Benjamin I then had to wait for the hospital's statutory six hours observation until I could hold him in my arms. It seemed like an eternity, and as I lay in the recovery room I cried tears of frustration and disappointment.

My friends had told me of their birth plans in the UK. Normal births, soft music and being able to hold and feed their baby moments after the birth. My first experience of giving birth was quite different, and was to be the first of many challenges raising children in a foreign land.

Six hours later a doctor brought Benjamin to me, and placed him in my arms.

'Well done,' he said. 'You have a very handsome son. He's doing well but there is just one small detail that I need to inform you of.' George was by my side, and we exchanged an anxious glance at the possibility of bad news. 'Benjamin was born with an extra thumb attached to the main thumb on his left hand,' the doctor explained, holding up Benjamin's tiny hand to show us. It was very small, but was indeed a complete thumb, with bone, ligaments and thumbnail. He explained that we would need to take him to an orthopaedic specialist when he was a few months old to have it surgically removed.

I was so grateful that he was healthy and had no other problems, so we decided we would worry about his thumb at a later date. For now I just wanted to hold my son in my arms. By this time our house group from church had arrived, and so had the pizza. My dream of feeding my son for the first time quietly, with just my husband by my side, was not to be. I awkwardly put him to my breast with four friends and their husbands looking on.

Initial motherhood was a mixture of exhilaration and desperation. I felt overjoyed at the arrival of my gorgeous little baby. He had big brown eyes, dark brown hair, and his cheeks were chubby and soft. However, I had never looked after a baby before and had no idea what to do. Breastfeeding was all-consuming as Benjamin would feed for hours, and then continue to cry. I tried desperately to make him use a dummy but he spat it out of his mouth so many times that eventually I gave up.

I realised motherhood was much more of a challenge in a foreign country. There were no health visitors, no mums' and babies' groups, and I felt lost and unqualified. Before Benjamin was born, I dreamed of having a large family with several children. A few months after his birth I reconsidered, and decided two offspring would be my limit.

One of the biggest difficulties was my change in routine. Before Benjamin was born, I was working full-time on the streets and in the *favelas*. Life was exciting and challenging, and George and I were like doctors on call, available to help anyone in need. Now, I was at home with a little baby who cried whenever I put him down, and I felt lonely and unfulfilled. I was thrilled to be a mother but was struggling to adapt to my new life. George continued to work full-time and often returned home late after visiting families in the *favelas*.

'I spoke to a woman today, George,' I said. 'She sounds like she needs a visit.'

George was using his computer and didn't look up. 'Oh, really, what's wrong?'

'She's really struggling at home with her little baby, and is feeling lonely and isolated.'

'No problem,' George replied. 'I'll pay her a visit. Just let me know her name, and where she lives.'

There was a moment of silence, and George looked up from his computer to see me frowning, and on the verge of tears.

'What's wrong?' he asked.

'It's me,' I exclaimed. 'I need a visit. You're always out helping others, and I'm stuck here at home by myself.'

George laughed, and I tried to laugh with him. We talked about ways I could be more involved in the project, at the same time as taking care of Benjamin. From then on I often accompanied George on visits and to the streets, taking Benjamin with us. I felt more involved, and he loved being the centre of attention wherever we went.

Chapter Twenty-three: A Real Home at Last

Those who are not looking for happiness are the most likely to find it, because those who are searching forget that the surest way to be happy is to seek happiness for others.
Martin Luther King Jr.[33]

'I'm so sorry,' Anita apologised. She placed an empty tin of tomatoes, full of steaming hot coffee, in my hand. 'We lost the cups in the flood last night.'

'Don't worry,' I replied, seeing her embarrassment. 'Your coffee always tastes good to me.'

I really enjoyed visiting Anita and Antonio. They were always so happy to see me, and Anita would squeeze me with delight whenever I arrived. They were two of the first people I had met when I arrived in São Paulo. I could hardly speak Portuguese, but they didn't seem to mind. Their shack was one of the poorest I'd ever seen, and was built alongside the sewage river that flowed through the *favela*.

There was a rickety porch area, with a steep step down from the road. The shack consisted of just one room. There was a living room

---

[33] Sir John Templeton, *Wisdom from World Religions* (Radnor, PA: Templeton Foundation Press, 2002).

area, with the kitchen in one corner, and behind an old torn curtain was the bedroom. The floor was dusty with no tiles or floorboards, and the shack was dark, and smelt of damp.

Anita had done her very best to make it feel like a home, and what most fascinated me were her plants. They produced a kind of berry that looked exactly like a hen's egg. Every time I visited her there were more and more eggs on the stalks, and this always made me amused.

Anita was short and tubby with a captivating smile. A few of her teeth were rotten and others were missing, and although she was in her fifties, she looked at least ten years older. A life of hardship and suffering was printed on her face, each wrinkle telling a story of daily struggles just to survive.

Antonio suffered with a condition in his spine, which meant he could only stand or lie down. His spine was fused together which meant he couldn't bend or sit. This hadn't stopped him from working as a carpenter, and a few of his handmade wooden toys hung from the ceiling by old bits of rope.

That day their smiles were not so wide. Once again the heavy rain during the night had washed away almost all of their belongings. Every time it rained hard Anita and Antonio's shack was flooded with water. They'd lost their furniture, clothes and kitchen equipment on many occasions. Almost all that they owned had been swept down the river, along with the rubbish, the sewage and the rats. Anita cried as she told me what had happened during the night.

'Antonio was asleep. The rain was so heavy it began to fill up the shack and I was scared we were going to be drowned. I pulled Antonio from the bed and took him out to the porch. The rain was so heavy, he had to stand there all night, with the water almost up to his waist.'

Antonio was pale and shivering, and I was concerned he'd caught a cold or even pneumonia. I struggled to contain my tears, unsuccessfully. A large teardrop rolled out of my left eye and trickled down my cheek. Antonio began to cry too. The three of us stood together in the living area and hugged each other tight.

How can people live like this? I thought. *This isn't living, this is just existing, from one flood to the next. How can I possibly help? Is there anything I can do to make a difference in these people's lives?*

That night I talked to George and we prayed together for Anita and Antonio, asking God for a solution. We decided we would talk to them the following week, and try to put together a plan to find them somewhere to live. First, however, we needed help. Their shack would be worth almost nothing, so we prayed for God to send us the money to buy them a new home.

A few weeks later we took a youth team from Northern Ireland to visit Anita and Antonio. They had asked to see our work in the *favela*, and Anita and Antonio were happy to meet them. We all squashed into their shack and told them their story.

'Anita and Antonio have lived here for many years, but Antonio was originally from a small town called Capelinha, in the north of Minas Gerais.'

'Yes,' Antonio added. 'I arrived in São Paulo thirty years ago, and have never returned home.'

God touched hearts that day. A few days later we received a message from the leader of the team to say they were sending a donation towards a new house for Anita and Antonio. My heart leapt with joy, and I began to imagine the two of them in a pretty little house, with eggplants and a sofa, pretty curtains and a wardrobe. I imagined a proper bathroom and coffee cups, and teatowels and a fridge. My mind was buzzing with ideas, and we prayed and thanked God for the miracle.

Soon after, our friends Roger and Lynda Everson, from Milton Keynes, came on one of their many visits. They too felt moved to help Anita and Antonio, and sent a generous offering a few days after their return home. They also shared Anita and Antonio's story with friends, and several people had made offerings too. We now had enough to buy a little house in a *favela*.

'George, we have enough money. Let's start looking for a house somewhere, far away from a sewage river.'

'There's just one problem, Cally,' George replied. '*Favelas* are illegal. We could buy them a house in a *favela*, and then in a few years time they'd lose the house if the *favela* is pulled down. We need to find them something more permanent.'

'But how?' I asked. 'We have 7,000 reais.[34] That's just enough to buy a decent little house made of bricks in a *favela*. If we want to buy a proper house, we need much more money than that.'

'There must be another way,' George said. 'Let's go and visit them tomorrow, and see if we can find a solution.'

The next day we arrived at their little shack with the good news.

'Anita and Antonio, we'd like to help you find somewhere else to live,' George said. 'Remember the people who visited you recently? They'd like to help buy you a house, and they've donated some money already.'

Antonio's eyes sparkled, and Anita burst into tears.

'Thank you, thank you, thank you,' she said over and over again for the next few minutes. They were both overwhelmed by the news.

'However,' George continued, 'we don't have enough money to buy you a proper house in São Paulo. So, I've been thinking, how would you feel about moving to Capelinha?'

'Oh, that would be wonderful,' Antonio exclaimed. 'That's my home.' Tears ran down his face as he thought about the possibility of finally returning home.

---

[34] Approximately £2,400 at that time.

'What about you, Anita? Would you like to go and live there?' George asked.

Anita didn't seem so sure. She'd never lived in Capelinha, and her home was São Paulo. It would be a big step for her, especially at her age, to start afresh in a completely different town, and a very different part of the country.

'I don't know,' she answered falteringly. 'Maybe it would be nice. It certainly would be lovely not to live in a *favela* anymore. And it certainly would be nice to live in a house that doesn't flood.'

'You don't have to decide today,' George told them. 'We just wanted to let you know of the possibilities and give you some time to think. We'll come back next week and see what you've decided.'

Anita hugged us the tightest hug ever, and we set off home, our hearts full of joy and expectation for what God was going to do. The next week they agreed to moving to Capelinha and we began to make plans. Our greatest challenge, however, in helping Anita and Antonio move to Capelinha was finding a means of transport.

'I can't believe no one is willing to help,' George said a few weeks later. 'How are we going to get Antonio to Capelinha if he can't sit in a car? It's an eighteen-hour drive. I've tried to hire an ambulance but no one wants to help. I just don't know what to do.'

George and his father had travelled there a few weeks earlier, and had bought them a house for 7,000 reais. It was a pretty little home, made of brick, with a small garden in the front. It was a proper house in a residential area, and just *happened* to be right opposite the house where Antonio's sister lived. It was perfect.

We told the good news about the house to our friends who had donated the money, and they sent another offering. This would help pay for the furniture, kitchen equipment, bedding and everything else needed to set up home. The documents were signed, and the house was painted and made ready. All that remained was for us to somehow find a way to take Antonio home.

'I think I've resolved it,' George said, a hopeful smile spreading across his face. He had just returned from visiting Anita and Antonio in the *favela*, and had come up with a solution. He had reclined the front passenger seat of our car to its lowest position, and asked Antonio to try to get in. With a little help from George and Anita he was able to wriggle into the seat, and said he was comfortable enough to travel in that way.

We were so happy, and relieved, that finally we would be able to organise their trip. A few days later George picked them up from the *favela* and brought them to our house for the night. The plan was for them to sleep at our house, and wake up early the next morning to begin the long journey to Capelinha. They would do half the journey that day, stay in a little hotel with George that night, and then continue the rest of the journey the following day. I really wanted to go with them, but needed to stay at home with Benjamin. He was just a small baby, and an eighteen-hour journey was not a pleasant thought.

I heard the engine of the car as they arrived in the driveway of our house. I rushed out to greet them, and could see their happy faces through the car window. Antonio slipped out of the passenger seat with more ease than I had anticipated.

George opened the boot of the car and took out their possessions. There were four plastic carrier bags full of clothes, and a canister of cooking gas. That was all they owned. Thirty years of living in São Paulo, and they left with just that. I was shocked, but then remembered all the times their shack had flooded. I felt so relieved that they were now going to live in a real house, and God had provided enough money to buy everything they needed.

I took Anita by the hand and led her into the living room. We sat and chatted and drank coffee, Antonio leaning happily against the wall.

'Antonio, would you like to speak to your mother?' George asked, with the telephone in his hand.

'My mother?' Antonio replied, taken aback. 'I haven't spoken to my mother for thirty years.' It was our turn to be shocked.

'Why so long?' I asked.

'I've never had a telephone,' Antonio replied, 'and it was impossible for me to get to the public telephone.'

George quickly dialled the number, and put the phone in Antonio's hand. Tears of joy flowed down his cheeks as he heard his mother's voice.

'I'll be there the day after tomorrow,' he assured her. 'I can't wait to see you after all this time. I love you, bye!'

He handed the telephone back to George, and began to half-walk, half-shuffle at quite a speed from one end of the living room to the other. I was concerned he was going to tip over, but he was so excited he couldn't keep still. We all laughed as he shuffled back and forth like a wind-up toy, shouting at the top of his voice, 'Oh, thank you, oh thank you,' until eventually he became tired, and slowed to a halt.

Anita and Antonio slept soundly that night. They had made a huge step in leaving the *favela* and starting this new adventure. They knew this was a chance of a lifetime and were willing to make this break. We also knew we were taking a risk. The Brazilians have a saying, 'You can take a person out of the *favela*, but you can't take the *favela* out of the person.' Would Anita and Antonio settle in Capelinha? Would Anita find it difficult to adjust to a town she didn't know and a family she had never met? Would she and Antonio give it all up, and return to live in a *favela* in São Paulo? Only time would tell. First there was a very long journey ahead, and a house to be made into a home.

'Can you imagine buying everything a person needs for their house?' George asked me, with a broad smile on his face. He had just arrived home after the eighteen-hour car journey back from Capelinha.

'We made a list, and went and bought everything,' George said. 'A TV, fridge, cooker, washing machine, pots and pans, bed, sofa, dining room table and chairs, wardrobe and chest of drawers, plates, cutlery, teatowels, bath towels.' George continued to tell me all that they had bought, and the list seemed to go on forever. 'It all went really smoothly,' George said. 'Antonio was quite comfortable in the car with the seat laid back. We stopped a few times to eat, and use the bathroom, and it went better than I could have imagined.'

'What happened when they saw the house?' I asked, desperate for information, trying to imagine the scene.

'They were overwhelmed,' George replied. 'They both just stood there with their mouths open wide and cried. Antonio's brother-in-law had painted the house, inside and out, and had made it look beautiful. Anita cried so much when she saw the garden. It's such a pretty little house, and in a quiet residential road. It's certainly nothing like a *favela*.'

'It must have been so amazing to see their reaction,' I replied. 'And what happened when Antonio met his family?'

'First he met his sister,' George explained. 'It was a wonderful moment for them both. They were in their thirties when they last saw each other. Then he met his mother, and she was so overjoyed to see him. I felt like I was watching a film, but it was real life. I left them with huge smiles on their faces, and I think they're going to be alright.'

So, our mission was accomplished, and Anita and Antonio were living in their new home. The following week they phoned to thank us and to say they were settling in, and really happy. They phoned almost every week for months afterwards to thank us.

Our main concern was how they were going to pay the bills. We sent them some cash, but it was difficult at first. They weren't used to paying water and electricity bills, as they didn't need to pay them when they lived in the *favela*. Now they had this expense every month, and Antonio couldn't work because of his disabilities.

Anita told us she was doing cleaning jobs and selling sweets at the traffic lights in the town. Eventually they told us the good news that Antonio had qualified for disability benefit. We were so relieved, as we knew that would make a big difference to their lives and their financial situation.

In 2004 Roger and Lynda came to visit, and made the long journey with us to visit Anita and Antonio in Capelinha. Ben was nearly three, and a very active child, so eighteen hours in the car was like torture for him, and for us. He said over and over again, what seemed like hundreds of times, 'I want to get out, I want to get out!' However, he survived the experience, and even quite long journeys felt short after that!

Sadly Anita died in 2017 from extremely high blood pressure, and several other health problems. At the time of writing, in 2020, Antonio is still living in the same house in Capelinha, and keeps in touch regularly on Facebook.

It is so wonderful to have been part of their story. Without help, Antonio would almost certainly be still living in abject poverty beside that sewage river. Anita certainly wouldn't have lived as long as she did, and it was wonderful that she had the opportunity to live in dignity in a proper home. I am so thankful for generous friends, a miracle-working God, and reclining front car seats!

Chapter Twenty-four: New Challenges

Home is where your pyjamas are.
Cally Magalhães

In the year 2002 I discovered I was pregnant again, and we were to have another son. We decided to call him 'Joseph' which means 'God added to the family' and in Hebrew, 'May God give increase'. We also gave him George's name as his middle name, like Benjamin, so he became Joseph George.

The day Joseph was born was 19 June 2003. Benjamin celebrated his second birthday the day before, so they are just two years and one day apart. I had hoped to try for a normal birth but my doctor felt it was too risky after one C-section. I didn't fight it this time, and I realised how my emotions after my first C-section had seriously affected my recovery. I was so upset that I couldn't have a normal birth with Benjamin that I took such a long time to heal, emotionally and physically. After Joseph was born I recovered much more quickly, and felt hardly any pain.

Joseph was a near-perfect baby. He rarely cried, and slept the whole night through at eight weeks of age. He was very handsome too, like Benjamin, but with blond hair and blue eyes that later turned brown.

Raising children as a missionary, and in another culture, is certainly a challenge. I could probably write a whole book on just that subject. Many of the situations I have faced happened to me for the first time in this new culture – like becoming a mother, for example. I had to learn all the vocabulary for pregnancy in Portuguese, and looking back it was quite a stressful experience.

During my pregnancy with Benjamin I needed to have my first ultrasound test. I went to the hospital and sat in the waiting room. I looked around me and saw that I was surrounded by women with stomachs of various sizes. Some women's stomachs were so huge they looked as though they were about to give birth in the waiting room. I hoped I wasn't going to be a witness to an emergency birth. I grabbed a magazine from the table by my side to stop myself from staring at the other women. The magazine was about interior design and there were different ideas for decorating babies' bedrooms.

At that time we were living with friends from our church. We were trying desperately to buy a house, and I wondered if we would move in before the baby was born. I looked at the photographs of nursery furniture in the magazine. There were beautiful wooden cots, wardrobes, rocking chairs and chests of drawers. I looked longingly at the furniture and wondered sadly if my baby would have to sleep in a cardboard box, as we needed to save all our money to buy a house.

A nurse shook me out of my daydream, and spoke to me so fast in Portuguese I had no idea what she was saying.

'*Você já esvaziou sua bexiga?*' ('Have you emptied your bladder?') she asked. The only word I recognised was *você* (you). All the other words were new to me.

'*O que?*' ('What?') I asked.

'*Você já esvaziou sua bexiga?*' she said again, at the same speed, with a hint of impatience in her voice.

'*O que?*' I replied again, now blushing with embarrassment, feeling my face turn bright red.

She sighed and said, '*Você... já... fez... xixi?*' ('Have you done a wee?') speaking rather more loudly than I would have wished and very slowly and clearly as if I was really stupid. At last I understood. She was asking me this because I needed to have a full bladder for the ultrasound test. I was now feeling extremely silly not to have understood, especially as most of the other pregnant women in the waiting room were now staring at me. By the time Joseph was born I was an expert in all the terminology, and the experience was quite different.

One day, just before Benjamin was to be born, George arrived home with some good news. His mother had given us a cheque for Benjamin's bedroom furniture. We had found a house and were moving in a few days later. We had enough to buy everything we needed. I didn't need to have been concerned after all.

I had several other challenges with my sons growing up in São Paulo. The first was in raising them to be bilingual. George and I realised they would speak fluent Portuguese simply by living and studying here as Brazilians. I wanted them to be fluent in English, and so I spoke in English to them from birth. There is, however, some ignorance in Brazil about bilingual children, and I faced some opposition. One Brazilian friend tried to alert me to the potential dangers.

'Oh no, you mustn't speak to them in English,' she said. 'They'll get confused, and then they won't be able to speak either language. They might not even be able to walk, and almost certainly they will have a stutter.'

I don't know where she had gained this information, but I chose to ignore her and others who gave me similar advice. Ben and Joe's first words were in English but after a while they swapped to only speaking in Portuguese. I continued talking to them in English, but they always replied to me just in Portuguese.

During a visit to the UK for three months they went to a small First School in Milton Keynes. It was a wonderful experience, and they were soon speaking in English at school. At home, however, they continued talking to me in Portuguese.

One night as I put them to bed, I expressed a little of my frustration.

'Ben, Joe, you know I was really hoping you would swap to speaking in English to me, now we're in England. You could do that, couldn't you?'

'Oh, Mum,' Ben replied, in Portuguese, 'you understand Portuguese. We're too lazy to speak to you in English.'

'I see,' I replied, tucking them into bed, stalling for time in order to come up with a reply. 'Well, I have an idea. If you swap to speaking English with me from now on I will take you to a toy shop before we go home, and buy each of you a really nice toy.'

There was an immediate reaction. Joseph sat bolt upright in bed and said, in English, 'So, Mummy, I have an idea. I would like to go the Lego shop. I've seen a toy there that I really want.' He continued talking to me in English for the rest of our time in the UK and still does to this day. Ben also swapped to speaking in English that night, and I confess that my unashamed blackmail worked. They both chose the toys they most wanted and I was a happy mum, with both of my sons talking to me in English.

Another challenge of living in a different culture was bedtime. In Brazil children go out with their parents in the evenings, even until late at night. It isn't unusual to see little children in restaurants at 11 p.m., running around full of energy, as if it was the afternoon. Babysitters are not common in Brazil, and I admit I didn't find it easy to adapt to this way of life.

One of the things that encourages late bedtimes here is that children only go to school for a few hours a day. If a child doesn't have to be at school until one o'clock in the afternoon, then it isn't a problem in their parents' eyes to keep them up late the night before. They can sleep the next morning without any problem, and so staying up late is normal.

We were part of a small group at our church in São Paulo, and two other families in the group also had young children. Our meetings began at eight o'clock in the evening, and we always took Ben and Joe with us. They played with the other children and ate with us, and then slept in the car on the way home. It wasn't ideal but I got used to it.

I learned the phrase, 'It's not wrong, it's just different,' before I moved to Brazil, and that helped me immensely. We're so conditioned to think that the way we've been raised or taught is the only way, or the right way, to do something. Every culture is different, and living in Brazil has taught me to be adaptable and accept other people's way of behaving and thinking. It isn't easy, but it is possible.

Being a missionary kid isn't easy, however. It often means many house moves, and adapting to different cultures. It means saying goodbye a lot, and not being sure where you fit in. When the boys were young, we travelled to the UK and went to stay with different friends in different towns around the country to share about our work.

One weekend we stayed with some friends in London and Ben became very attached to their two cats. When it came to the time for us to leave, he cried and wanted to stay. In the car I tried to comfort him, saying we were going home (back to our other friends' house in Milton Keynes which was our base for the three months). By now Ben was distraught, and said, 'That's not home, that's Pete and Wendy's house.'

'Well, it's home for now. Where's home, anyway?' I asked, pondering the question more for myself than anyone else. 'I've got it. Home is where your pyjamas are!' That seemed to settle it, and has been our family saying ever since.

I have also had many opportunities, as a missionary, to show my sons, in very practical ways, that God answers our prayers. They have had the opportunity of seeing God's provision on many occasions. When Ben was about five years old I didn't have any money to buy food for dinner that night. I wanted to buy some bread, milk, eggs and sausages but my purse was empty, and so was the bank account.

'Ben, come here a minute. I want to pray with you about something.' Ben came running into the lounge and we sat on the sofa together. He cuddled up beside me, and I hugged him tightly and stroked his hair. 'Ben, I don't want you to be worried, but I don't have any money at the moment. I need to buy some food for us to eat dinner after you get back from school. Can we pray together and ask God to help us?'

'OK, Mummy,' Ben replied, and shut his eyes.

'Dear Lord, thank You that you're always with us,' I prayed, 'and that You're such a faithful God. Please, Lord, we need some money to buy some food.'

Before I could continue Ben opened his eyes, jumped off the sofa, and exclaimed, 'Mummy, I have some money in my moneybox. You can use that. I'll go and get it.'

I reached out and took Ben's hand before he could run out of the lounge.

'Ben, wait. That money's yours for you to buy toys, and you've been saving it for ages. You don't have to give it to me to buy food.'

'That's OK, Mummy, I want to,' he said, and ran off to fetch the moneybox. He arrived a few moments later, out of breath from running so fast. He knelt down in front of the sofa, and turned his moneybox upside down. Coins scattered all over the sofa and we gathered them up, and counted them one by one.

There were ten reais and five cents, enough to buy what I needed for dinner.

'Thank you, Ben,' I said, pulling him towards me for a big, tight hug. 'You're amazing. Now we need to thank God, don't we?'

I began to pray, 'Thank You, Lord for this money. Thank You that you bless us so much. I pray, Lord, that You will help us to help others too, like the street children...' I was about to continue when Ben interrupted me.

'Mummy, we need to give some of this money to the street children.'

I stopped and looked at my son. I realised that even at such a young age he had an awareness that others were in greater need than us.

'You're right, Ben,' I answered. 'Let's count out a tithe, that's 10 per cent of what we have, and we'll buy some food for the street children next time we go to see them.'

I found an envelope, and Ben placed a one-real coin inside and I wrote 'For the street children' on the front. We tipped the coins into a plastic bag, and a few minutes later set off for the long journey to school. We lived in a small town called Araçariguama at that time. It was fifty kilometres from the centre of São Paulo, and Ben studied at a bilingual school in the afternoons, about forty kilometres away.

My heart was overflowing with joy as I drove Ben home from school that day. Things were really tight financially but God, once again, had provided. I was so grateful to Him, and to my son for his generosity. My plan was to stop at the little supermarket in Araçariguama on the way home and buy the things we needed for dinner.

Suddenly the toll fee sign loomed into my view above the motorway, a few hundred metres ahead.

Oh no! I exclaimed to myself. I had forgotten I would need to pay the toll fee. *Now what am I going to do?* I had the bag of coins, but if I used them then I wouldn't be able to buy the things for dinner. With a heavy heart I stopped at the tollbooth, and started to count out the coins. I had to use almost all we had, and now I certainly wouldn't have enough to buy food.

It took me a couple of minutes to count out the money, and I was embarrassed I didn't have any notes. However, I was also very grateful for my bag of coins as at least I could pay the toll fee. Ben was already dozing in the back of the car and oblivious to what was happening. I continued driving along the motorway, thanking God for the coins, but feeling sad we wouldn't be able to buy food. I wondered how we were going to eat dinner that night.

We arrived home about twenty minutes later.

'Ben, wake up, we're home,' I called softly, as I walked around the car to help him climb out of his car seat. He had only slept for about half an hour, but it was enough to have recharged his batteries. He jumped out of the car and I unlocked the front door of the house. He raced inside, grabbed a toy, and ran ahead of me into the kitchen. I felt so sad I'd spent all his savings on the toll fee, and couldn't bring myself to tell him. I wondered how I could improvise to make dinner from the few ingredients I had in the food cupboard.

'Mummy!' I heard Ben call out. 'Mummy, come and see!' I walked quickly into the kitchen, and saw Ben looking at the table in amazement.

I was overwhelmed as I looked at the table. Everything that we were going to buy was there, and more.

'Look, Mummy, sausages, milk, eggs and bread. Rice, spaghetti, flour, butter and sugar.' Ben recited the names of the food proudly, not realising the significance of each one. There was also a note from my mother-in-law, and I stared at it as Ben danced around in delight.

'Dear Cally, I bought a few things for you at the supermarket. Love Mum.'

I made dinner that evening, praising God for His provision, and for hearing our prayers. I looked forward to telling George what had happened when he arrived home later that night. As I put Ben to bed that evening, I snuggled up beside him, and told him about what had happened at the tollgate.

'God is so faithful, isn't He, Ben? We can trust Him for everything. He knows all that we need. He not only provided the money for the toll fee, but He provided all the food we needed, and some other things as well. Goodnight, Ben, love you so much.'

'Goodnight Mummy, love you too,' Ben said softly, turning onto his side, and cuddling up with his toy dog, Pingo.

'Oh, Mummy,' he added.

'Yes, Ben, what is it?'

'And don't forget to spend that money on the street children.'

Chapter Twenty-five: The Eureka Moment

We are all faced with a series of great opportunities brilliantly disguised as impossible situations.
Chuck Swindoll[35]

In the year 2004 we met Renan, while working with street children in the centre of São Paulo. He was fifteen years old, and his face was lined and tanned from so many years of street life. His smile was enchanting, and his face lit up every time we arrived. It felt like God knitted our hearts together from the moment we met him. He called us '*mãe*' and '*pai*' ('Mum' and 'Dad') and we desperately wanted to help him leave the streets.

We visited his family, who lived in extreme poverty in a *favela*. The house had just one room where the family lived and slept – his mother, his older brother (who was a drug user) and his brother's girlfriend. There was no room there for Renan.

A few months after meeting him, he was imprisoned in the youth prison, in the same unit we had visited in the year 2000. We had been praying that Renan would leave the streets, and he did, but not exactly in the way that we had hoped. During a fight he pulled

[35] James Harrison, *Monday's Message* (Bloomington, IN: WestBow Press, 2012).

out a huge knife and attempted to stab another street-dweller. He didn't notice that right beside him was a police officer, who promptly arrested him, and he was sent to the youth prison.

A street-kids organisation that was accompanying him lost their funding shortly after, so they invited George and me to visit Renan every week. We were delighted, as we had longed to start work in the youth prison and now was our chance. We were allowed to talk to him by himself, pray for him and continue to build the relationship with his family. These visits enabled us to work together with him and the youth prison staff to help him find a different future, far from the streets and crime.

That was how our work in the youth prisons began. Almost every week the social workers or psychologists in the unit knocked on the door of the little room where we held our meeting,

'I am so sorry to interrupt,' they would usually say. 'Is there any possibility you could talk to another boy who lives on the streets? He also doesn't have any visitors. Would that be possible?'

The list grew longer as each week went by, and after a few months we were helping at least twenty teenagers in the same unit as Renan.

In the year 2006 we officially opened an NGO[36] with the name 'Associação Águia' (The Eagle Project). We prayed for a long time for the right name for the organisation. Eventually both George and I both felt 'The Eagle Project' was the one. There are many references in the Bible to the eagle, and we felt it was relevant to our work with the boys.

Isaiah 40:31 says:

> but those who hope in the LORD
> will renew their strength.
> They will soar on wings like eagles;

---

[36] Non-Governmental Organisation.

they will run and not grow weary,
they will walk and not be faint.

The boys we work with need to renew their strength, learn to reach their potential, and not grow weary of trying to do the right thing. We also heard of a legend telling of how the eagle renews itself when it reaches the age of about forty years. The legend is an inspirational story of rebirth, renewal and new hope. However, it's just a legend, and my hope is that our boys will tell their own real-life stories of overcoming and restoration.

In the year 2006 we began working in various units of the youth prison in different areas of São Paulo. We sent many teenagers to rehabilitation centres for treatment of their drug addiction, and many others we helped return to their families.

However, there was a problem. Most of the boys didn't want to go from the youth prison straight to a rehabilitation centre. They felt like they were still in prison, and often they ran away after a few days and returned to live on the streets. We lost contact with them and this left us frustrated and sad, as we so wanted to help them to find a different future.

We realised that in order to continue helping these boys, we would need psychiatrists and psychologists to be part of our team. Without the necessary funds to make that happen I began to pray for an alternative way to help these boys. I was in search of something radical that would help them change while they were in the youth prison, and as a result wouldn't reoffend on their release.

In the year 2011 a friend from Milton Keynes sent me a book called *The Geese Theatre Handbook*.[37] It is about a group based in

[37] Clark Baim, Sally Brookes, Alun Mountford, (eds), *The Geese Theatre Handbook: Drama with Offenders and People at Risk* (Hook: Waterside Press, 2002).

Birmingham, England, that works in prisons. As I read this book, and learned of their amazing project using psychodrama, I realised that all my theatre experience from the past was buried. How could I have led drama workshops or directed plays in Brazil, when I didn't even know how to speak the language?

Now, with my Portuguese becoming fluent, I felt able to unearth it and use it for our work in the youth prisons. I started writing a new project using psychodrama.

Would this be the answer for these young men's lives? I felt like this was my 'eureka' moment! I called the new project in Portuguese *'Sonhar e voar – quebrando as correntes'.* Literally translated this means 'Dream, fly and break the chains'.

The teenagers we work with do have dreams of a different future, but they feel so limited by their poverty and lack of opportunities, they don't believe it's possible. They're bound not only by the *physical* chains that bind them, but also by the chains of habits, behaviours and ways of thinking and reacting. These need to be broken, and through the project we encourage them to 'fly' and achieve their potential.

Some friends from São Paulo who are psychodrama therapists encouraged me to do an introductory course in psychodrama. I realised psychodrama was everything I was dreaming of to help these teenagers. Psychodrama offers a way of working with individuals and groups to help them think differently, and look at their world from a new perspective.

Also at that time I learned about Restorative Justice,[38] and heard about the very effective programmes in various countries working with offenders and their victims. Restorative Justice treats justice

---

[38] See Howard Zehr, *The Little Book of Restorative Justice* (New York: Good Books, 2015).

restoratively instead of punitively. It helps the victim to come to terms with their trauma or loss, and this is so important. It also helps to restore the offender, encouraging empathy, forgiveness and restitution.

I began to realise it would be possible to use the methods of both psychodrama and Restorative Justice, as the two overlap perfectly. I talked to George about it.

'This is incredible!' I exclaimed. 'Through psychodrama the boys can go into all different roles as their victims, their victim's relatives, police officers, their mums, their girlfriends. I think this could really help.'

I presented the project outline to one of the coordinators of the youth prison, and shortly after it was approved.

'Would you prefer to work here with the serious and extremely serious reoffenders,'[39] the director of the unit asked, 'or in another unit with first-time offenders?'

'Oh, definitely the reoffenders,' I replied. 'Surely they're the ones who need the most help to not reoffend?'

In Brazil, any young person under the age of eighteen who commits an offence will stay in prison for a maximum of three years, and then will be released. They may have committed extremely serious offences, but won't be transferred to the adult prison. This gave us even more of an incentive to work with the boys who are considered multi recidivists. I knew we would be helping these boys find different futures without continuing in crime and violence. I also knew we would be helping save many potential victims from trauma, injury, or death.

In 2012 we began the psychodrama sessions at the youth prison. I invited two psychodrama therapists, Beatriz Petrilli and Carolina

---

[39] Multi recidivists.

Maroni, to lead the sessions, and at the same time I began a postgraduate course to become a psychodrama therapist. I was so excited to be learning about psychodrama at last, and made the most of every lecture. I had to learn a whole new set of Portuguese vocabulary, as well as write homework assignments in Portuguese.

This was a very stretching time for me as I was quite happy to talk in Portuguese, but not to write it. I was even more challenged when at the end of the first year I discovered we were expected to write a thesis and present it before a board of examiners.

I felt extremely grateful to be working weekly with Beatriz and Carolina in the psychodrama workshops. I remember vividly their first day at the youth prison. They both were visibly frightened as we waited to be introduced to the new group of boys.

'You do realise that you don't need to be scared at all?' I said.

'Really?' Beatriz asked.

'Really,' I replied. 'You may not believe in God, or have a strong faith, but I do, and I know for sure He called me here to Brazil to work for Him. So, if I'm in centre of God's will, then that's the safest place in the whole world. And if you're with me, then you're in the safest place too.'

They both looked at me and breathed a huge sigh of relief. They looked at each other and grinned, an expression of trust and confidence spreading across their faces.

I was their assistant for the first year, and I was able to put into practice everything I was learning during the course. Being part of the sessions was like a dream come true, as Beatriz and Carolina were so spontaneous and used the techniques of psychodrama with such creativity. The sessions were exciting and the scenes were tense, as the boys experimented with the roles of their victims and victims' relatives.

In the second year, I had the experience of directing the sessions with the support and help of Beatriz and Carolina, giving me the opportunity and confidence to learn 'on the job'. I met Laisa Teixeira, a young Brazilian psychologist from my psychodrama postgraduate course. She was brilliant, spontaneous and dynamic, and shared my same passion to work with adolescents, and help them find a new future. She joined the team in 2013, and has worked with me ever since.

We soon realised that psychodrama was an extremely effective tool in working with these adolescents. As we began to evaluate our work, we also realised that if the boys participated in at least ten sessions they were much less likely to reoffend.

One boy, of Japanese descent, was chosen to take part in our project. It's unusual to meet Asians in the prison system in Brazil, and this boy was considered a very serious reoffender who had even tortured his victims. His social worker brought him into the room and left him with these words, 'This one, only by the grace of God.'

We began to work with him and the members of the group, and gave them various opportunities of experimenting with different roles. During the final evaluation we asked the Japanese boy what he thought of the psychodrama sessions.

'Cally, the truth is that when my psychologist talks to me it's just "blah, blah, blah". However, when I went into role as my mum, when I *felt* what she feels when I reoffend, now I know I will never reoffend.'

This young man is now married with two children and hasn't reoffended. I realised he could have listened to his psychologist for years, and would never have reached the insight that he found by going into the role of his mother. I also realised the importance of being given a second chance. We don't ask the boys about their crimes, or read their records. We make this our policy as a team so that we remain impartial and don't run the risk of judging them for their crimes or behaviour. That is a very different experience to what they are used to and they respond so positively to this 'unconditional love' that we have waiting lists for all of our groups.

Another boy, Alexandre, was put in the youth prison twice for stealing up to ten motorbikes a day. He also robbed people at gunpoint as they withdrew money from the ATM. He was chosen to take part in the psychodrama sessions, but wasn't too keen on the idea. He wanted to continue in crime, and had no intention of changing his behaviour.

One session the group made up a scene where Alexandre was the *owner* of a motorbike, not the thief, and was sitting at a traffic light waiting for it to change. The other boys in the scene burst in to steal the motorbike, imaginary guns pointed at his head, and I shouted: 'FREEZE!'

I turned to Alexandre, and said, 'What are you thinking right now, how are you feeling?'

In the role as the victim he looked at the robbers and shouted, 'No, you can't steal my motorbike! This is my motorbike. I bought it with my money, and I need it to go to work.' Alexandre told me later that at that moment he realised what he had been doing wrong. Suddenly he came to his senses, and realised that he was doing exactly that same thing to up to ten people per day. He suddenly became aware that he was robbing honest people who were just trying to get to work.

'Would you tell me your story, right from the beginning?' I asked him recently, when we met for lunch.

'Well, I suppose the problems all started with my mum,' he began. 'She was adopted, and my grandmother gave her more attention than her other children. As a result, her brothers and sisters were all jealous of her. Then she got pregnant at the age of fourteen, and I was the baby. I still don't know who my father was. It was just some guy she had sex with. So, when I was born my grandmother raised me, along with my mum and her brothers and sisters.

'We lived in a really poor neighbourhood and life was very hard. My aunties, that's my mum's elder sisters, they raised me too. Right from when I was really young everybody hit me; my mum, my grandmother, my aunties and my cousins. It was really hard at home, and as I was being beaten so much I behaved the same way, and started hitting the children at school. I realise now I would just lash out in anger for what I was going through at home.

'I was suspended from nursery school for trying to strangle another kid with a shoelace. That's when I was two and a half. Then when I was in second grade I lost control and hit a kid around the head with a desk, and then stamped on his head. I don't know why I did it, I was just so angry with everyone. I got beaten for that too. After that I wasn't allowed into school unless I was with an adult member of my family. I had to arrive fifteen minutes after the start of school and leave fifteen minutes after everyone else had gone home.'

'How did that make you feel?' I asked.

'I was the bad boy, and so my life continued the same way. At the age of ten I learned how to take motorbikes apart to sell the parts. Then at the age of eleven I stole my first motorbike. My grandmother tried to stop me by locking me in my room. She used to call me "FEBEM".[40] I thought, "Well, if my name's FEBEM then I might as well behave like the kids there."'

---

[40] *Fundação Estadual para o Bem Estar do Menor.* Literally translated: The State Foundation for the Well-being of Children. This was the name given to institutes for badly behaved or needy children and adolescents, which later became the youth prisons I work in today.

Alexandre paused and took a deep breath. Tears began to well up in his eyes and roll down his cheeks. I put my arm around his shoulder.

'I'm so sorry, that is so hard,' I said.

'Then I just went from bad to worse,' he continued. 'I was arrested at the age of fourteen and taken to the police station, but that time I didn't get put in prison. One day my friend and I did seven robberies. We robbed supermarkets, cars and motorbikes. When the police turned up I was sitting with my friend on one of the motorbikes we'd stolen. They shot my friend in the head and the leg.'

'Did he die?' I asked.

'No, his motorbike helmet saved him, but he was badly hurt.' He went on, 'When I was twelve I got my first tattoo.'

Alexandre lifted his trouser leg to show me. The tattoo covers the whole of his lower leg, and is of a carp fish.

'What does it mean?' I asked.

'It's to "show off" all the different things I "achieved" in the world of crime. I did it to show I "belonged". The older guys doing crime had everything, and I admired them and wanted to be like them. They had money, respect and girls, and that was what I wanted too.

'I was put in the youth prison, and then when I was released I got sent back after just two months. Later I escaped from the prison, but got caught and they sent me back again.'

'What happened? How did you escape?'

'I planned it really carefully. I pretended I was in agony with appendicitis. The guards were really worried about me, and instead of waiting for an ambulance one of them took me to the hospital in his car. They tried to handcuff me with my arms behind my back but I pretended it was too painful in that position, so they handcuffed me with my hands in front of my body.

'When we arrived at the hospital I pretended I needed to use the bathroom. I'd put a T-shirt under my prison T-shirt, and had practised for weeks taking off the prison T-shirt with my hands clasped together, as if wearing handcuffs. Now it would be more difficult for them to identify me. The guard was standing in the doorway of the bathroom with the door half-shut behind him. I stood behind the door, then kicked it so hard he went flying and fell to the floor.

'I ran past him at high speed, and out of the hospital entrance. I just kept running and running until eventually I heard the sirens of police cars behind me. By this time I was on the side of the motorway, and could hear a police officer huffing and puffing as he tried to catch up with me.

'I turned around and saw him try to jump over the central reservation. He missed and slammed his shin into the metal bar. He swore loudly and grabbed my legs and I fell to the ground. Several police cars arrived at the scene, and the motorway was closed, all because of me.

'They took me to the police station and I got beaten up really badly that day. They sent me back to the youth prison, and I had to stay in solitary confinement for forty days. After that I met you and the team from The Eagle Project.

'That day when I did the scene of me on the motorbike, but as the owner not the robber, I couldn't sleep that night. I realised I needed to change or I'd be in prison the rest of my life, or dead.

'When I was released I decided to do a hairdressing course. I already cut the other boys' hair in the youth prison, and everyone said I was good. I asked my family to help me pay the first month of the course but no one wanted to help me. They didn't believe I could change. I begged them and eventually had enough money to pay the first month of the course.

'I began cutting my friends and neighbours' hair and saved enough money to pay for the second month. I opened my first salon in my grandmother's garage and put aside enough money to rent my own salon, and then The Eagle Project helped me, remember?'

'Yes,' I replied.

'That was so cool. That very kind American man from your church helped buy the barber's chairs, forty-five towels and seats for the customers. Wow, what a blessing that was!'

'Alexandre, I'm so privileged to be part of your story. It's so amazing to see the young man you've become, and what an example you are to so many other young boys.'

Alexandre has recently opened a new salon and completed a course, sponsored by The Eagle Project, to teach others to be barbers. His dream is to help the boys in his poor neighbourhood and the boys from the youth prison. He knows it's possible to change, and has joined us several times at the youth prison, talking about his transformation and doing barber's workshops for the boys. He is like a son to me and calls me 'Mum'. We meet up for lunch about once a month, and I am so blessed to see how well he's doing.

Sadly, most of the boys have similar stories of difficult family situations. Wanderlei also had a difficult childhood and was expelled from school at the age of eleven. Then he was expelled from his next school for beating up another student. His parents separated and he began to smoke weed, steal and sell drugs at the young age of twelve.

'What made you start doing all these things?' I asked him.

'My older brother was already involved with a life of crime, and I admired him. I wanted to be like him, so I started too. He's in prison now, and has been for nine years.'

'How many times did you go to the youth prison?'

'Three times. I was in the youth prison for four years, from the age of fourteen to eighteen. Looking back, it was such a waste of my adolescent years.

'While I was in prison, my younger brother was murdered. He was only sixteen. He went out stealing one night, and was shot. That was one of the worst days of my life, when my dad came to the youth prison to tell me he was dead.

'I had a dream that night that a woman was speaking to me. She was a Christian, and she told me that God had closed *my* grave, but opened another. I woke up and understood that the dream meant that my brother had died but that I was meant to live. That dream certainly made me think more deeply about my life.'

'How did the psychodrama sessions help?' I asked.

'It was that session when Antonia talked about her house being burgled. When she said her sons were crying because their video game had been stolen, I turned to you, do you remember?'

'I do remember, yes.'

'And I said, "Wow, I feel really bad now, that's what I used to do." It made me realise the consequences of my actions and I decided to change.'

'You know you're my hero, don't you?'

'No, why?'

'Remember the football game?'

'Oh, yes, that day was crazy! We were allowed out of the youth prison to play football against another youth prison unit. Everything was going smoothly until suddenly an armed gang burst into the stadium, and held up the guards at gunpoint. They were shouting for us all to escape and the boys just legged it out of there, as fast as they could.'

'Why didn't you go too?'

'I knew I could, but I stopped for a split second and thought about it. If I'd escaped I'd almost certainly have been recaptured, and then I would have had to serve my whole prison sentence again. I knew I had just a few weeks left in the youth prison, so I folded my arms and stood there.

'Now look at me,' he said. 'I'm nearly finishing radiology at university, and have a full-time job. I'm so glad I didn't run away.'

Wanderlei is sponsored by one of our board members, who pays his university fees here in São Paulo. He is an example of a young man whose life has been completely turned around. He would almost certainly have continued in a life of crime if he hadn't received help and decided to change. He has accompanied us in the youth prison on two occasions to talk to the boys about his story and encourage them to dream of a different future. He is like a son to me and calls me 'Mum'.

When he was just about to start his first work experience, he phoned me.

'Mum, I'm starting my work experience as a radiologist in a hospital next week.'

'Wow, that's fantastic,' I said.

'Yes,' he replied. 'I am really excited to put into action all the things I've been learning. But can I ask you a favour? I need white clothes and shoes to wear at the hospital. Do you think it would be possible to help buy some, please?'

'Of course,' I answered. 'Let's meet up this week and get what you need.'

A few days later, we went to a shop in São Paulo that sells uniforms, and Wanderlei chose what he needed. I took photos and it was a wonderful moment of celebration.

As we stood waiting to pay, I said to the lady who was serving us, 'This is my son.'

She looked at Wanderlei who has dark skin and dark hair, and then looked at me with my pale skin and blonde hair.

'Oh?' she said, obviously a little confused.

'Yes, he's studying radiology at university,' I replied, a huge, proud smile on my face.

'Congratulations,' she said to Wanderlei.

I glanced at Wanderlei and saw him physically 'grow'. His shoulders went back and his chin lifted high. At that moment I knew he felt loved and accepted. Young people like him often just need someone to say, 'You're mine.'

A few months ago he sent me a message.

Hi Mum, guess what happened? I was on the bus and a young woman was begging. I felt God touch my heart to help her. I had just a few coins in my pocket so I gave them to her. I remembered you, Mum, and the way you help people.

I felt so encouraged when I read this. My desire is that the boys we help will not only get jobs or go to university, but they will love others and be a blessing wherever they go. Also, I am beginning to realise the powerful link between psychodrama and the gospel. When Jesus died on the cross, He took our place, and became the sacrifice that we needed for the forgiveness of our sins. That amazing act set us free. In psychodrama, when someone puts them self in the place of another, and really understands what that person feels, then freedom comes. They are then free to live, to give and be all that God intended for them to be.

Chapter Twenty-six: Being in the Right Place at the Right Time

If you think you're too small to make a difference, you haven't spent a night with a mosquito.

African Proverb[41]

Six million children in Brazil live in abject poverty, which means families exist on less than a dollar per day. Many of these six million children live in São Paulo.

'*Cestas básicas*', or food parcels, can help to keep a family alive for several days. They cost from between £15 to £25 (depending on the size), and contain basic foods like rice, beans, flour, sugar, oil, pasta and coffee. There's no meat, milk, eggs, fruit or vegetables but there is enough food to keep people alive. A *cesta básica* can make a huge difference to a family who have little or nothing to eat.

I have often talked about *cestas básicas* on my visits to the UK,[42] and many people have donated money to provide a regular food

---

[41] Fr Kevin E. Mackin, *Enjoying God's Gifts* (Bloomington, IN: WestBow Press, 2018).
[42] I try to visit the UK every two or three years to see family and friends, and thank my supporters.

parcel for families in need. After one such visit, a very kind friend called Sheila Williams decided to give an offering for a food parcel. My friends Roger and Lynda Everson were due to visit me in São Paulo, and during their last Sunday at church she called them aside.

'Please give this money to Cally,' she said, pressing a £20 note into Lynda's hand. 'Ask her to buy a food parcel for a family in São Paulo. You pray together, and ask God to show you who you should give it to.'

A few weeks later Roger and Lynda arrived, and told me the story of Sheila's offering. We prayed and asked God to show us who should receive it. While we were praying, a woman called Rosemeire came into my mind. She had five children, and was extremely poor.

I'm sure she'll be very happy to receive a food parcel, I thought, *and blessed to know the money came from so far away to buy it.*

We bought the food parcel at the local supermarket, and drove into the centre of São Paulo to deliver it. I was excited to know we would be blessing Rosemeire, but never imagined the reaction she would have when she saw the parcel.

She was living in a deserted apartment block where many families had made their home. These places are often old office blocks or flats that are disused for some reason. Sometimes they are quite well administrated and run by an organisation called 'Sem Teto', literally translated 'No Roof'. There is a rigid procedure for residents and visitors to enter the building, and no drugs or firearms are allowed.

However, they are still dangerous places to live. The electricity and water are pirated, and devastating fires occur every year in these buildings. The lifts are out of order as there's no official electricity, and residents have to walk up and down several flights of stairs every day. One family I visited lived on the eleventh floor, and it was a challenge to walk up all those stairs to see them, especially when I was pregnant. The staircases are littered with human excrement, as there are no official bathrooms in the building. They are dingy and subhuman places that many call 'home'.

Armed with the food parcel, we knocked on the door of the apartment. After a few seconds Rosemeire came to the door. She was a middle-aged woman with long, dark brown hair, typical of most Brazilian women. She had a tired and worn-down face with sunken eyes. Before I could say a word she exclaimed, 'Oh! Now I know God is real!'

Surprised but delighted to hear her reaction I asked, 'Why are you saying that, Rosemeire?'

Her eyes filled up with tears as she replied, 'This morning I put the last rice in the pan to feed my five children. I have no food in the house. I cried out to God, "If You're real, then please help me. Please send someone to help me today."'

Roger placed the heavy food parcel in her outstretched arms, and I translated what she had just said for him and Lynda to understand. We all filled up with tears, and realised the miracle God had just done. Actually, the miracle He had been preparing for weeks before. First Sheila felt she should give the money. Then, weeks later we prayed about who should receive it, and sensed it was for Rosemeire. Then, we arrived on the very day she prayed for help.

Wow! God is so awesome, in His timing and His love for His children. What a privilege to be part of His plan for this earth. How amazing to be the answer to someone's prayer!

A few months later I visited a *favela* to take food parcels for three families I was helping. This *favela* is one of the poorest I have ever visited. Built alongside a sewage river, the stench of the stagnant water and the stink of the piles of rubbish hit me hard as I arrived that morning. Dogs wandered around aimlessly and lines of clothes that had been washed that day were strewn from shack to shack.

The sun was hot on my neck as I walked along, carrying one of the food parcels. They're too heavy to carry more than one at a time and the plastic slid through my fingers as I struggled not to drop it. Children ran barefoot between the shacks and men sat chatting on rickety stools and upturned wooden crates. A group of boys were playing football, somehow avoiding the dog dirt on the dusty ground. I looked more closely at the ball and saw that it was made from socks tied together.

Brazilians play football wherever and however they can, I thought to myself.

A huge variety of sounds met me as I continued walking. Babies were screaming at the top of their lungs, funk was blaring for all to hear, mixed with the hubbub of conversations and laughter between neighbours and friends.

Kites were flying high in the sky above the *favela*. Kite-flying is a common pastime in Brazil, and not just for children. It isn't unusual to see teenagers or adults flying kites, especially men. It's almost like a sport. They coat the kite string with glass powder, and attempt to cut the other kite-flyers' strings, on purpose. Then the race begins to see who can find the kite before anyone else and claim it as their own.

The shacks were made of assorted pieces of wood, some sturdier than others, but all extremely poor. Most were hanging precariously over the sewage river below, and I wondered how they stood up to the storms. I remembered Anita and Antonio, and gave thanks that they were living in a proper little house, and not in a *favela*.

The families greeted me with smiles and hugs. I handed the food parcel to Antonia, the mother of one of the families, and she quickly took it inside her shack.

'Do have more food parcels, *Tia*?' one of the boys asked me.

'Yes, I have two more for two other families.'

'Do you need some help to carry them?'

'Yes, please,' I replied enthusiastically, and we went back to the car, several other children also anxious to help me. The boy and his friends gallantly placed the other two parcels on their shoulders, and we returned to their families. This time most of the adults along our way had turned to stare at me, and I greeted each one, 'Good morning, God bless you,' and continued on my way.

We delivered the parcels and then, linking their arms in mine, the children took me back to Antonia's shack. We sat squashed together on a very old, stained sofa, and I drank a small cup of strong, sweet black coffee. The drinking water in the *favela* is not very clean, but it would be rude to refuse. I always pray for God to protect my stomach and have never had any problems so far.

'I have a job now,' Antonia explained. 'I'm working as a cleaner doing night shifts in a hotel.'

'That's so good,' I replied. 'You needed a job, didn't you?'

'Yes,' she answered sadly. 'Since my husband died things have been so hard. It's so good I have a job, but there's just one problem. I have to leave the children alone here all night. I lock them in, and worry there might be a fire or an accident and I won't be here to help them.'

I shuddered at the thought. Her youngest child was two years old, and the eldest just ten. It was such a huge responsibility for a child that age and legally he was too young to look after his four younger brothers and sisters. What would happen if there was a fire? They would be trapped inside the shack with no adult to help. It felt like a tragedy waiting to happen.

What should I say? I thought to myself. *Here's a poverty-stricken woman trying to provide for her family. Who am I to criticise and say she shouldn't leave them? What solution can I find?* My only suggestion was for her to leave a key with a relative or trustworthy neighbour. At least then, in the event of a fire or accident, someone would be able to get into the shack to rescue the children.

We chatted some more, and I played cat's cradle with two of the girls. Then it was time to leave, and I offered to pray. Everyone gathered together and held hands. Some older boys who were neighbours were lying on the bunk beds, and they jumped up and joined in. They removed their caps respectfully, and held hands in the circle. I prayed a simple prayer of blessing and peace, provision and protection. I always aim to pray for people whenever I can. When we pray then the supernatural power of God intervenes and His love comes in.

I hugged everyone goodbye and walked out into the hot midday sun.

Midday sun, I said to myself as a memory jolted my mind. Me, dressed in a 1930s costume, performing in *Cowardy Custard*. It was the Noël Coward musical at my dancing school in East Grinstead, and I was singing that the only ones to go out in the sun at midday would be 'Mad Dogs and Englishmen'.[43] It felt like another life and another world, so removed from this one. I was jolted back to reality as cries of *'tchau'* ('goodbye') and *'até logo'* (see you soon) accompanied my departure.

'Excuse me. I'm so sorry to trouble you. Please could I talk to you in private?' A tiny old woman stopped me as I walked out of the *favela*. She stood in my path and beckoned me to follow her. She led me into her shack, and I was shocked at the lack of furniture. There was a small single bed, which filled one side of the tiny room. On the other side were a battered old fridge, a small rusty cooker, and a food

---

[43] 'Mad Dogs and Englishmen' is a song written by Noël Coward (1899-1973) and first performed in *The Third Little Show* at the Music Box Theatre, New York, on 1 June 1931, by Beatrice Lillie.

cupboard slanting at 45 degrees. The room smelt musty, and the floor was dusty beneath my sandals. There were gaps in the corrugated iron roof and a bucket on the floor to catch the rain. The room was hot like a sauna; sweat ran down my spine like water from a tap.

'I'm so sorry to trouble you,' she said again. 'I was wondering if you could give me a food parcel too. I have nothing. Look!'

She opened the fridge, and indeed there was almost nothing there. No food or drink, just a small half-empty packet of coffee. She led me to the slanting food cupboard, and slid open the door with some difficulty. It was empty. No food at all.

'Of course,' I said gently, and her wrinkled face broke into a wide smile.

'I don't have any more food parcels but I can run up to the supermarket. I'll buy you what you need. Let's make a list.'

About half an hour later I returned with several carrier bags full of food. She was waiting just outside her home, and we went in together with the shopping.

I must tell her about Jesus, I thought, and knelt down in front of her on the floor. She was so tiny I didn't want to tower over her, and there weren't any chairs or a sofa. I looked into her eyes and took hold of her hands.

'Do you know Jesus?' I asked.

She smiled, and gently squeezed my palms.

'Oh, yes,' she replied slowly, but with real conviction. 'This morning I prayed to Jesus. I asked Him to send one of His servants to help me.' She paused. 'And He sent you.'

A surge of joy rose up inside me, and my eyes brimmed over with tears. I hugged her tightly, and she laid her head on my shoulder and cried with me. Time stood still for a few moments as we held each other, both of us thanking God together. What a privilege to be in the right place at the right time. What an awesome thought that I could be the answer to someone's prayer.

I remembered the saying that I love so much:

As one person I cannot change the world, but I can change the world of one person.[44]

I really can't change the world, but I can try each day to change the world for one person. What a privilege.

---

[44] Anonymous.

Chapter Twenty-seven:
We Laughed Until We Nearly Died

> If you believe in a God who controls the big things, you have to
> believe in a God who controls the little things. It is we, of course, to
> whom things look 'little' or 'big'.
> *Elisabeth Elliot*[45]

'Cally, André is dead!' Rhiana's voice shook as she spoke, and her
tone was urgent. Rhiana was working with us on the streets, and was
phoning to say that André had died. He was a friendly boy, seventeen
years old, who had lived on the streets for many years. He had a
wonderful sense of humour, and always greeted us with a big hug
and a huge smile. I will never forget him picking a headlouse off my
forehead just as it was about to disappear into my long hair to lay its
eggs.

Like most of the street kids in São Paulo, he had a family, and a
mum who loved him. He had dropped out of school when he was
about twelve, a similar story to many of the street children. The
classes at the state schools are often huge, with about fifty children

---

[45] Elisabeth Elliot, *Let Me Be a Woman* (Carol Stream, IL: Tynedale House Publishers Inc, 1976).

in each. His attendance was sporadic, and when he was at school he couldn't keep up.

The regular fights when his dad arrived home drunk late at night made it hard for him to wake up for school the next day. Sleep was a luxury, in-between the beatings for him and his mum. Hiding in the wardrobe with his little brothers and sisters, he dreamt of a different life, far from this hell. Soon he was attending school less and less, and spending more and more time on the streets. There he could be free. No one told him what to do, and he didn't have to go to school anymore. He had a group of friends he called his 'family' and his mum didn't seem to miss him at home. Eventually she threw his dad out on the street, so she didn't need André to try to protect her anymore. It wasn't easy living on the streets in the winter, but sniffing glue took the edge off the cold. He begged for food, and pickpocketed passers-by when he needed money.

'What happened?' I asked, tears welling up in my eyes. I liked André, and I was sad his short life had to end so soon. We hadn't seen him for several weeks, and were wondering if he was OK.

'I've no idea,' Rhiana replied. 'I just know the wake will be this evening, and the burial tomorrow.'

I still haven't got used to the speed at which people are buried in Brazil. Someone dies, and by the next day they're buried. It doesn't feel right, somehow. It seems I need longer to process my thoughts, and my grief. I'm also not good at going to sleep really late, and certainly don't like staying up all night. But this is the culture and I've chosen to embrace it.

I began to realise we were in for a long, sleepless night.

It was late afternoon and we had just finished visiting the street kids. We were on our way home but George turned the car around and we went back into the centre of the city to André's house. Our hearts were heavy, and we drove in silence, wondering what could have happened to our young friend.

We arrived at the house to find André's mum crying uncontrollably, and his little brothers and sisters wailing like babies. Our presence seemed to calm things a little, and we sat with the family, their heads on our shoulders as we all cried together.

Little by little we were able to piece together what had happened. André's dad had received a phone call saying his son was dead, and calling him to identify the body. He went to the mortuary, signed the papers, and informed the rest of the family. That was all the information the family had gained. No one knew how André had died. Was he murdered or did he die in an accident? What, where, how? No one knew any details at all.

The phone rang, breaking the tension. It was the funeral director informing André's mother that his body had arrived at the cemetery and we could proceed to the wake. We stuffed many more people than the legal limit into our car, and set off. We arrived about half an hour later and walked sadly and slowly up the hill to the long, low building. There were about six small rooms, each with a coffin, and family members gathered around each of the bodies.

André's name was on the door of one of the rooms, so we all filed in ceremoniously to say our goodbyes. André's mum went in first, accompanied by the funeral director, and then one by one we followed. When I arrived at the foot of the coffin (open, as is the custom in Brazil), I heard a gasp. André's mum was staring at the body, and exclaimed in a loud voice, 'That's not my son! That isn't André. This boy is black. My son isn't black!'

'There, there, madam,' the funeral director comforted her. 'It's difficult to accept when one of our loved ones dies. Please just remain calm, and take your time to come to terms with this sad loss.'

'No,' she cried louder. 'You don't understand, this isn't my son! This isn't André. There's been a mistake.'

'Madam, are you sure?' the funeral director questioned. 'His name is on the door.'

'I don't care what it says on the door,' she was now shouting. 'This isn't my son!'

We all looked at each other in disbelief. This boy's skin indeed was black, but his face was not dissimilar to André's.

'Madam,' the funeral director said very calmly, 'we need to be absolutely certain. Is there any identifying mark on your son's body that we can check, just to be sure?'

'Yes!' she exclaimed. 'He has a tattoo of a little bluebird on the back of his neck.'

Without hesitating, the funeral director climbed on top of the coffin. Placing one foot on each side he bent down, and cleared the daisies from around the neck area of the body. He grabbed the boy's shoulders, and heaved up the upper part of the boy's body.

Dead people are heavy, I thought.

'Madam, quickly, please look for the tattoo,' the funeral director shouted. We all craned in to look at the boy's neck. There was no tattoo. No bluebird.

'See,' André's mum cried out, 'there's no tattoo. See, I told you it wasn't my son.' She now burst into tears of a different kind, dancing around the coffin, jumping for joy. We all clapped and laughed, and cried and danced.

The mourners in the waiting area outside gathered at the door and peered into the room. What a scene to behold. A whole family and their friends were celebrating the death of their loved one?

Bewildered faces pressed their noses against the glass. No one in the room cared. We laughed and hugged each other and continued to dance and clap for several minutes.

When our laughter subsided, we sat down exhausted. I was overwhelmed with all the emotions of the last few hours. First sadness, then confusion, then shock and then joy. After a few minutes, André's mother asked, 'But if this isn't André, then who is this boy? And where is André? And why did his father sign the papers saying he was dead? I'm going to kill him myself!' We were very confused, but nothing took away our joy. We politely asked to enter each room just to check André wasn't there, and then we drove home, laughing at the strange turn of events. The only thing that clouded our minds was our concern for the whereabouts of André. Why had he disappeared? Was he alive? Or would we discover that he really had died?

Later that night we discovered the truth about what happened that day. André's father had indeed received a phone call saying André was dead. He had gone to the hospital to identify the body but the problem was he was blind drunk. He was crying so much at the news of André's death, he didn't even look properly at the body, and signed the papers.

A few weeks later I was sitting on the street, and chatting to a group of street-kids. One of the girls, Bella, turned to me and said,

'*Tia*, have you heard about André? He's in prison.'

'In prison, in prison?' I jumped to my feet, and shouted out loud, 'That's amazing, fantastic, wonderful news. André's in prison. Praise God, what wonderful news.'

Bella looked at me strangely. I was jumping up and down, praising God that André was in prison?

Realising her confusion, I sat down and explained, 'Bella, a few weeks ago André disappeared. We heard he was dead and we went to his funeral but it was all a mistake, and he wasn't dead after all. We didn't know where he was, and we were concerned for his life. Now you tell me he's in prison, so I know for sure he's not dead. I'm not happy he's in prison, but I'm so glad he's alive.'

'Oh, now I understand, *Tia*,' Bella replied. 'You had me worried for a minute. I thought you'd gone mad!'

Chapter Twenty-eight: Restorative Justice

Forgiveness is the key to unlock the chains that bind me.
Cally Magalhães

'I've just finished the most amazing course[46] on Restorative Justice,' I told my team. 'Laisa did the course with me, and it's going to be so useful for our work with the boys in the youth prison. The course was divided into two parts and taught over twelve days, three days each month.

'This course was incredible. We were encouraged to look at how we deal with our anger, in what ways we're aggressive, and how we communicate with others. We went back into our past when we were victims of aggression or abuse, and learned how to forgive and move on.

'The second part taught us how to facilitate restorative circles, where offenders and victims have the opportunity to meet and talk about what happened. It was so powerful I asked if I could learn more about Restorative Justice to use it with our boys. The director

---

[46] CDHEP Centro de Direitos Humanos e Educação Popular de Campo Limpo (The Campo Limpo Centre for Human Rights and Popular Education), cdhep.org. br (accessed 22.5.20).

of the course suggested I join their team working in the adult prisons where they teach the same course.

'I've agreed to work with them one day a week in an adult male prison about forty-five minutes from my house,' I continued. 'It's in the opposite direction from the centre of the city, so the journey's going to be less stressful as I won't have to drive in the rush-hour traffic.'

'That is certainly a blessing,' one of the board members agreed.

'I'm so excited about this. I so long to see prisoners set free from their anger, hatred and revenge, all the things that keep them imprisoned in their past and unable to move on. I know this is going to be transformational for our work in the youth prisons.'

The following week I began working at the adult male prison, teaching a group of twenty prisoners. I was working with Maria, a sixty-three-year-old Catholic nun, who had a wealth of experience working in prisons. I was keen to learn from her, and curious to see how the course would help the men.

The prison is situated in the countryside, and there is no direct access by public transport. That means visitors have to walk about a mile and a half from the nearest bus stop.

We arrived early in the morning, I parked the car, and Maria gathered up the equipment she had brought with her. She had a box with folders, one for each student, name badges, lead pencils, coloured pencils and paper. She also had brought several plastic bags full of modelling clay. I was impressed at her strength to carry all that weight on the bus and train. We walked from the car park to the entrance of the prison.

'We have to wait here,' Maria explained, 'and hand in our documents. They have our details, and they'll phone through to the reception to say we've arrived.'

I had time to look around me. The prison was surrounded by huge walls, all topped with spirals of barbed wire. Guards stood at their guard posts at intervals along the top of the walls, wielding large guns, with grim expressions on their faces. Everything was grey except for a huge blue gate about 100 metres away.

'How many prisoners are here?' I asked Maria.

'The prison was built for about 750 men,' she replied, 'but there are about 1,500, apparently. Overcrowding is a huge problem in Brazilian prisons and one of the main reasons for the riots.'

I knew about this from watching the news. In the last decade alone, the prison population has nearly doubled and hundreds of prisoners have been murdered. Tensions escalate, and during the riots prisoners are stabbed, strangled or decapitated.

It was a winter's day in São Paulo and I felt a chill run down my spine, despite my several layers of T-shirt, cardigan and jacket. Silence hung in the air. No birds were singing, the sun wasn't shining and the clouds threatened rain.

'You can go in,' the guard at the entrance gate said with little expression in his voice. 'They're waiting for you at reception.'

We walked across the car park in the direction of the huge blue gate.

'Maria, let's pray,' I said.

'Of course,' she replied. We stopped walking and I linked my arm in hers.

'Father, thank You so much for this opportunity to serve You. Please prepare the hearts of the men who are going to take part in the group, and use us as instruments in your hands. I pray this in Jesus' name. Amen.'

'Amen,' Maria agreed, and we continued to walk towards the main gate. A guard peered through a small opening, and opened a side gate for us to enter.

'We need to give in our documents here as well,' Maria explained. We handed them to a woman behind the reception desk who smiled and seemed happy to see Maria again. She wrote down our names and document numbers in a large visitors' book.

'Take off everything metal that you're wearing,' she said. I began to take off various items, including my watch, earrings and jacket.

'Take off your shoes as well,' she said, and beckoned for Maria to go through the metal detector. It was like a doorframe, with sensors at different levels to detect any metal objects.

'That's my false hip,' she said, laughing as the machine beeped loudly, and a light went on at hip level as she walked through.

Now it was my turn, and I walked through apprehensively, hoping I'd remembered to remove everything metal. The machine kept silent, and I smiled at Maria in relief as we put everything back on. We waited a few minutes, and then a guard opened the next gate, and accompanied us as we crossed a small courtyard.

A guard allowed us through the next gate into the building, and we gave in our documents once again. This was the third time we'd been asked to show our documents in the space of about fifty metres. Here there was a larger X-ray machine, and we had to remove everything metal again, and pass through another doorframe. Maria's false hip lit up and beeped once more. Then we had to place the equipment we had brought with us into the X-ray machine, together with our shoes. Maria bent down and undid her shoelaces with some difficulty.

I heard a loud noise behind me, and turned and saw the gate opening. Two burly guards appeared, pulling a cart laden with boxes of vegetables. It passed through the gate in front of us with no apparent inspection. I laughed quietly to myself.

How ironic, I thought. *The sixty-three-year-old Catholic nun has to bend down and take her shoes off to put them in the X-ray machine, yet a whole cart-load full of boxes just passes through with seemingly no inspection at all. Those boxes could be full of weapons, mobile phones and knives, and no one would know.*

'Can I help you, Maria?' I asked, quickly tying my shoelaces after taking my shoes out of the X-ray machine.

'No, don't worry, Cally, I'm used to it,' Maria replied enthusiastically. I was full of admiration for this woman who had left home at 5:30 that morning, and travelled by train and bus to meet me.

I have a lot to learn from Maria, I thought to myself.

We passed through another gate into an open courtyard, flanked by kennels with several vicious-looking Rottweiler dogs. I linked my arm in Maria's as they snarled at our legs through the wire fence. We walked quickly across the courtyard and into the building in front of us, and handed our documents to a guard sitting at a table.

There was a strong smell of bleach, and I noticed that one of the prisoners was cleaning the floors. I knew he was a prisoner because he was wearing brown trousers and a white T-shirt, the official prison uniform. He was using a '*rodo*', a kind of windscreen wiper attached to a broom handle, and covered with a floor cloth. He worked quickly and efficiently, and I wondered how many years he'd been doing that job.

Maria led me along the corridor to an office and introduced me to the director of the prison. There was a murmur of chatter, of phone calls and staff sharing information.

'Welcome back, Maria, and we're happy to welcome you too, Cally,' the director said. 'I have prepared the list of men who will take part in the group. You'll both come every Wednesday until December, is that right?'

'Yes,' Maria confirmed. 'The first group will be ten sessions, until the end of September. Then we'll begin the next group with another ten sessions until December.'

'I hope you can do something with them,' his colleague chipped in. 'If it was up to me, I would send them all for organ donation.' He laughed in a way I found menacing and my stomach churned at the thought. I didn't feel it would be wise to challenge him on my first visit, but his words made me determined to bring restoration to these prisoners' lives, including the staff members if possible.

We left the office and passed through five more doors and gates, until finally we arrived at the block where we would teach the course. This was a very different scene from when we were passing through the administration area. There was a strange murmur of voices, which sounded like a snoring, sleeping giant. I couldn't understand where the noise was coming from until I peeked through a hole in the wall beside us.

There was a large courtyard area full of hundreds of men, most of whom were walking in a large circle around the edge of the courtyard. Some were ambling slowly, chatting and smoking; others were walking purposefully, using the time to exercise. I wanted to stop and watch, fascinated by the scene, but I heard a gruff voice behind me.

'Move along, move along, you can't stop here,' the guard barked.

'Oh, I'm sorry,' I replied, and we continued walking to the block in front of us. The men were waiting on a stairwell behind a gate, and our arrival seemed to cause a hubbub of talking and shouting.

'*Camiseta, camiseta,*' ('T-shirt, T-shirt') the men nearest the top of the stairwell shouted to their fellow prisoners.

'Why are they shouting that?' I said in a loud whisper to Maria.

'It's considered highly disrespectful not to be fully dressed in front of women visitors,' she whispered back. 'The men have lots of different rules amongst them that have to be obeyed.'

'But it's so cold,' I replied. 'Why don't they already have their T-shirts on?'

'I've no idea,' she said, 'but now I understand why so many of them have pneumonia.'

I tried not to stare but my eye caught sight of a boy near the gate. I was so shocked I struggled to keep my mouth from falling open. He stared back at me through the bars, his eyes wide open in a look of desperation. He looked no more than fourteen years old, and certainly not old enough to be in an adult prison.

How can that boy be eighteen? I thought, remembering the boys in the youth prison, most of whom looked much older than him. *He has to be at least eighteen to be here, but he looks so young.* I wanted to cry but managed to hold back the tears. I tried not to think of the abuse he would almost certainly be facing in that place, at the mercy of the other men. I smiled at him and put my thumb up, and he smiled back at me, his eyes welling up with tears.

The men who were to take part in our course were allowed through the gate into the school area, and we followed behind them. The gate was shut behind us and we were locked in. Breakfast had been delayed so we were all ushered into the library area, and prisoners on breakfast duty gave out bread rolls and coffee. One of the men offered me a cup of coffee and I took it gratefully. There were about fifty men in this small space, as well as a couple of female teachers.

As soon as I put the cup to my mouth and the coffee touched my tongue I realised I had made a big mistake. This wasn't coffee. It was 'cevada' or barley coffee and it was disgusting. It tasted like nothing I'd ever tasted before, and now I had no choice but to drink the whole cup. I didn't want to be rude so I drank it, hoping I wouldn't throw up.

Thank You, Lord, that I am not in prison, I prayed. *How would I survive without proper coffee? There's no way I would be able to stay in prison drinking that stuff for any length of time.*

The library was small but well-stocked, with a variety of reading books and textbooks. I learned later that reading is important to many of the men to relieve their boredom. I chatted to a couple of the men, and felt the eyes of the forty-eight others boring into my back. I must have been a source of curiosity for these men, with my blonde hair, blue eyes and fair skin.

I knew I was in a potentially very dangerous situation. If the men wanted to, they could overwhelm me, Maria, and the other teachers in an instant. However, I felt totally at peace and soon breakfast was over. We followed the men to our classroom, which was at the end of a long corridor. There were three other classrooms that were also beginning to fill up with students. Their teachers were all middle-aged women, wearing white coats over their clothes. All the prisoners were dressed alike with brown trousers, white T-shirts and flip-flops.

'Is everyone allowed to study?' I asked Maria.

'Oh no,' she replied. 'Only about fifty men in each of the two wings have the privilege. That means just 100 men out of 1,500 prisoners. It's considered a huge privilege, as each day of study is one day deducted from their prison sentence.'

What a shame, I thought to myself. *It would be an amazing opportunity for these men if they could all study. Then they would have more chances for employment after their release.* I realised I had a lot to learn about the prison system in Brazil.

Some of the men helped us make a circle with the chairs, and Maria and I greeted each man with a smile and a handshake. After taking the register and explaining the course we did a name game, and the men were obviously beginning to relax and enjoy themselves.

Without warning the man from the office who had talked about organ donation appeared in the doorway.

'Roll call,' he announced gruffly, and proceeded to shout out each prisoner's name in a monotonous tone of voice. Each man replied and shouted their prisoner number, in an equally monotonous voice. He left, and the men were visibly relieved.

'It's so cold here,' one of the men said. 'We wake up in the morning and there's mist hanging over our heads in the cell.'

'Socks are a luxury,' one of the other men said, lifting his legs to show his bare feet. He was wearing only flip-flops. I looked around the circle, and saw that hardly any of the men were wearing socks, even though the temperature was about 8 degrees C.

'And there are only cold showers,' another said.

'The cells are so overcrowded we have to sleep in shifts. There isn't space for us all to lie down at the same time. We tie our sweaters and ourselves to the bars, and sleep sitting up or even standing up,' another added.

I looked at each of these men, and wondered why they would keep reoffending and returning to this hell of a place. I realised more than ever their need to be restored, and helped to find real freedom in their lives.

Maria and I handed out a lump of modelling clay and a piece of cardboard to each man.

'Find a comfortable position sitting in your chair, feet flat on the floor, with your eyes closed,' Maria instructed the group. Then she told them to imagine themselves walking down some steps and sitting down in a room with a large screen before them. On the screen were images of a difficult experience in their lives. She gently encouraged them to think of a situation where they were a victim, and remember the details of where they were, what happened etc.

Then after a few seconds they walked back up the stairs in their imagination and opened their eyes. This was an exercise intended to help the men concentrate and recall the situation in their minds for the next activity.

'Now, using the clay, make a sculpture that represents this situation, using the cardboard as your base. You have several minutes to work so take your time,' Maria instructed the group.

Some of the men began to break the clay into pieces with great enthusiasm and roll it and mould it into different shapes. Others rolled the clay back and forth in their hands, some staring into space, others staring at the clay. One by one the clay began to be transformed into different shapes, as each man worked silently and purposefully. Their faces were lined with concentration as they tried hard to make the clay into something meaningful.

After about fifteen minutes Maria said softly, 'You have about five minutes to finish your sculpture,' and handed a black felt-tip pen to each man. 'When you have finished, please write the emotion you feel most strongly at this moment on the cardboard.'

I walked around the circle and was amazed by the creativity of each man. Some had made whole scenes of families, including furniture and other objects. Others had formed the clay into guns and knives with bodies lying beside them. One man had made a coffin, and another the bars of a prison cell. Each sculpture told a story, and after they all finished, Maria encouraged each one to share with the group.

Bruno, a tall black man, about twenty-five years old, was the first to speak. His sculpture was of a gun.

'When I was ten years old I got a gun, and went to shoot my stepfather,' he said. 'I intended to kill him but my mother stood between us and screamed at me to stop.'

Bruno was speaking slowly as if every word that he uttered was difficult to speak. He took a deep breath and continued, 'My stepfather told her to choose. Him or me.'

Bruno stopped again. The room was silent as we all waited for him to continue. Bruno's fingers continued moulding the gun as he spoke, pressing the clay harder into the cardboard.

'My mum chose him.' Bruno paused, and breathed in again. 'They sent me out of the house that day and I never returned. I had nowhere to stay so I ran to the streets. I felt like my life wasn't worth living anymore. I was just ten years old. I got into crime, robbing people at gunpoint, and was put in the youth prison many times. I was just so angry and sad I didn't know what else to do. Now I'm here, and will be for a long time.'

Just one big tear rolled down Bruno's cheek. He licked it as it trickled over his top lip and into his mouth, swallowing hard, drying his cheek with his forearm. The man next to him patted his shoulder and Bruno tried to smile, grateful for the gesture.

'Thank you for sharing your story, Bruno,' Maria said gently. 'We know that required a lot of courage. Who would like to go next?'

'I will,' said Everton, an overweight man of about thirty years old, with a chubby, smiley face. His sculpture was of a rope in the shape of a noose. 'I was just five years old, and my mum and dad had a terrible fight. My dad left the house and went to the bar next door. My mum locked me and my little brother in our bedroom.' He paused, took a deep breath, and continued. 'We didn't know what to do so we just went to sleep. The next day we woke up, and our mum had committed suicide.'

Everton's face contorted, his eyes closing tight as he remembered the pain of that day. Tears rolled down his face, and the man next to him put his arm around his shoulder and squeezed it tight.

'My life's been a mess ever since. I couldn't deal with the pain and the trauma, and just took out my anger on everyone. Now I'm here, and it isn't the first time I've been in prison.'

The group nodded in understanding. I wondered if I would have enough emotional strength to hear twenty stories like this. Each was so tragic, and I didn't know if I could take any more. I took a deep breath and prayed, *Lord, this is really hard. I need to be strong. Please help me.*

One by one the men explained their sculptures and told us their stories. Deaths and murders of family members, people they had killed, one who killed the man he found in bed with his wife, betrayal, abandonment and abuse. At the end of the session Maria explained that this was probably the hardest one of all, and that in the following three sessions we would be working with activities based around their stories. We gave everyone an opportunity to say how they were feeling, and they thanked us profusely for going there to help them.

We said goodbye and hugged each man as we went around the circle. Some were like stiff pieces of wood, and I wondered how long it was since they'd received a hug, if ever. Others hugged me tightly, and thanked me for being there.

We left the prison, passing through all the security doors and gates again, retrieving our documents, and saying goodbye to each guard on our way. At the final reception we were signed out, and we left the main gate and walked into the car park. The cold wind hit me in the face and I was grateful for it. Tears had begun to fall from my eyes and I pretended it was the wind, not wanting to cry in front of Maria.

I drenched my pillow with tears that night, each man's story passing like a film through my mind. I prayed for each one, and couldn't wait for the next session the following week.

Each session brought more freedom. We taught on forgiveness, on how to forgive ourselves as well as others. We taught about the circle of violence and crime, and how so often we dehumanise the people who hurt us. We explained the need to rehumanise our aggressors, realising that they too are human and have problems of their own.

We did an activity where each man was asked to think of a person who had hurt them or harmed them, and then make a 'map' of their life. They had to write down where the person lives and works, who they live with, their likes and dislikes, hobbies and activities. We also encouraged them to write down what the aggressor thought of them at the time of the offence, and what they think now.

The men all began the activity except for one young man, Charles, who was sitting with his pencil in his hand, staring into space.

'Charles, can I help you?' I asked. 'Are you able to think of an aggressor?'

Charles looked at me sadly and replied, 'Cally, there are so many.'

'Try to choose just one,' I encouraged him gently.

He then said something that moved me deeply.

'You know, Cally, when I came to this prison I decided that on my release I would murder my ex-wife. She abandoned me, and so did my father, so I decided I would murder her. Now I've done this course I realise it's not all her fault, and she isn't all to blame. She has problems too. I've decided I won't murder her after all. I've learned to forgive her.'

I swallowed deeply, and gave Charles a big hug.

'Wow, that's so wonderful, Charles, that's real forgiveness.'

At the end of that session Bruno shared what had happened to him in the past few weeks, as a result of the course.

'You know I told you I tried to kill my stepfather, and I was sent away from home? Well, my wife visits me every week, and I've been telling her about this course and what I've been learning. I told her I've learned about forgiveness and that I've been able to forgive my mum.

'You'll never guess what she did. She went and found my mum, and told her I've forgiven her. She said my mum burst into tears, and told her she's regretted sending me away all these years. My mum said she loves me, and is so sorry for what she did.

'Then this last Sunday my wife brought my sons to visit me. One is nine and the other is seven. For the first time ever in their lives we had a conversation. I sat on the ground with them, and they told me about their Taekwondo classes. We talked about school and football and all kinds of things. I've always been so screwed up with my own pain and problems that I never actually talked to my sons. Sunday was one of the best days of my life.'

The group clapped and cheered, and Bruno smiled from ear to ear. He looked so different from the bitter, angry young man we had met in the first session.

'That's wonderful news, Bruno,' I said. 'God's restoring not only you but your relationship with your family members too.'

During another session I explained the Circles of Violence and Reconciliation,[47] devised by Olga Botcharova, a Russian psychologist and expert in conflict resolution. She lived and worked in Bosnia-Herzogovina during the Bosnian war, and her teaching is transformational. She explains that we need to move out of the circle

---

[47] Olga Botcharova, 'Implementation of Track Two Diplomacy: Developing a Model of Forgiveness' in Raymond G. Helmick, SJ, Rodney L. Petersen (eds), *Forgiveness and Reconciliation: Religion, Public Policy, and Conflict Transformation* (Philadelphia, PA: Templeton Foundation Press, 2001).

of violence, anger and revenge, and understand our traumas and pain. Only then will we be able to move into the circle of forgiveness and reconciliation. I had the privilege of working in Mostar, Bosnia for one month, as a volunteer, shortly after the war ended. I was able to understand first-hand the importance of forgiveness and reconciliation in a nation torn apart by war and the atrocities of ethnic cleansing.

A man called Fabrício, a drug trafficker in São Paulo, Belo Horizonte and Curitiba interrupted me and said, 'Cally, I now realise I don't have to kill anymore. I've murdered so many people. I even kill from here.' He looked down at his feet in shame, as if he understood the consequences of his actions for the first time. 'I just make a phone call, and someone on the outside murders the person for me. Now I realise that every one I kill is someone's father, or husband, or son, or brother.' He paused and looked up at me and smiled. 'I now understand I don't need to kill anymore. I can resolve my conflicts in a different way.'

I didn't know whether to dance, or cry, or leap in the air. I was so overjoyed to hear this breakthrough for this hardened criminal.

'That's amazing to hear, Fabrício, and the good news is that when you leave here you'll have a huge impact on those around you,' I said. 'Can you imagine all the people who know you as a murderer? They will be amazed and moved to see you showing empathy instead of killing people. Praise God!'

I had the privilege of leading this course with six different groups of men, in that prison. The transformation was incredible. At the end of the first four sessions of working on their trauma, represented by their sculpture, we held a ceremony. They wrote a new emotion on their piece of cardboard, based on how they felt after these first four sessions.

Each man came forward slowly, and tipped their sculpture into a sack. Then they read out the emotion they had written when they first made their sculpture, and then the emotion they had just written.

'Hatred. Forgiveness.'

'Anger. Relief.'

'Abandonment. Forgiveness.'

'Revenge. Joy.'

'Pain. Freedom.'

Each man read the words aloud until everyone had thrown their sculpture into the sack. The atmosphere in the room was one of unity and fellowship as each man said the words he had written. No one laughed or made any comment. Some of the men were visibly moved, and wiped tears from their eyes as they threw their sculpture into the sack.

'After the session today, Maria and I will stop on the side of the road, and we will throw the contents of this sack into the undergrowth,' I explained, holding the sack open in front of me. 'This is a way of showing that these sculptures, and all they represent, is in the past. We don't forget the things that have happened to us, but we can choose to forgive, or begin the process of forgiving, and move on.' We joined together in a circle, our arms around each other's shoulders.

'Thank you for your courage,' Maria said. 'It takes a lot of strength to get in contact with our past and our traumas. Many of you have been in prison more than once. We all know you didn't reoffend because you like it here and wanted to return. If we don't find our way out of the circle of violence, we will keep thinking and behaving the same way and will keep returning to prison for the rest of our lives.'

We left the prison and drove along the forest road. After a few hundred metres I stopped the car, and took the sack full of sculptures into the undergrowth. The trees and bushes were still wet from the morning dew, and I inhaled deeply, savouring the smell of the wild flowers around me.

What a perfect place to throw these clay sculptures, I thought to myself. *So much pain and trauma was infused into this clay, not only from the lives of the men, but of their families and victims too. What a privilege to be part of their stories.* I shook the sack violently, praying for their freedom and transformation, and returned to the car.

'That was powerful,' I said to Maria.

'Yes,' she replied. 'Restorative Justice is powerful.'

What an amazing privilege to have worked in this prison, and to have learned more about Restorative Justice, and the power it has to transform lives. I even had an opportunity to challenge the staff member who spoke of using the men for organ donation. We were nearly at the end of one of the courses, and he asked how it was going.

'It really is transformational,' I replied, and told him Charles' story, without mentioning his name. 'He had every intention of murdering his ex-wife after his release,' I explained. 'During the course he was able to forgive her, and now has no intention of murdering her anymore.'

The member of staff stood with his mouth open as he heard my words.

'I didn't realise that was what the course was about. That's truly amazing,' he said. 'Congratulations. We need this course in every prison in Brazil.'

Chapter Twenty-nine: Acceptance

I lift up my eyes to the mountains -
where does my help come from?
My help comes from the LORD,
the Maker of heaven and earth.
(Psalm 121:1-2)

Forgiveness is *really* difficult. I learned that lesson when I realised I needed to forgive my first husband. I never imagined I would have to find an even deeper degree of forgiveness again.

In 2014 things started to go wrong between George and I. His dream was to study at university, so he started a degree in Sociology and Politics, in the centre of São Paulo. It was a four-year course so we knew it would put a strain on our family. However, Benjamin was thirteen and Joseph was eleven, so we felt they would cope.

I wasn't prepared for what the next three years would bring. George was forty-one, and a mature student. I don't want to write here all that happened between 2014 and 2017, but it was a very challenging time. In April of 2017 I asked George to leave. Not only was it the end of our marriage but also of our working relationship with The Eagle Project, which we had founded and built together. There was no way he could continue to be involved, so he left the NGO officially a few months later.

It was a very dark time as I worked through my second divorce. I wrangled continually with what I could have done differently. I wondered if I gave too much attention to the project and to our sons, and not enough to him. I questioned how I had failed as a wife. If I had challenged him sooner, maybe things wouldn't have reached this point.

Every day for the first three months after he left I woke up relieved, thinking it was just a nightmare. Then, moments later I realised I was awake and it was real. A deep sadness overwhelmed me, and I pressed in hard to find God's peace. Often I couldn't even find the words to pray. There was just a silent continuous cry in my heart of: *GOD. HELP!* He was so real to me on a daily basis, and it was a very different experience from my first separation when I hardly knew Him. The *Footprints in the Sand* poem became a daily reality to me:

One night I dreamed a dream.
As I was walking along the beach with my Lord
Across the dark sky flashed scenes from my life.
For each scene, I noticed two sets of footprints in the sand,
One belonging to me and one to my Lord.
After the last scene of my life flashed before me,
I looked back at the footprints in the sand.
I noticed that at many times along the path of my life,
especially at the very lowest and saddest times,
there was only one set of footprints.
This really troubled me, so I asked the Lord about it.
'Lord, you said once I decided to follow you,
You'd walk with me all the way.

But I noticed that during the saddest and most
troublesome times of my life,
there was only one set of footprints.
I don't understand why, when I needed You the most,
You would leave me.'
He whispered, 'My precious child, I love you and
will never leave you
Never, ever, during your trials and testings.
When you saw only one set of footprints,
It was then that I carried you.'[48]

I felt as though God was indeed carrying me through this storm. There were times when I felt like dying, but I knew I couldn't give up because of Benjamin and Joseph. Also, I knew I would survive this. I knew that one day I would smile and laugh again.

I continued working, at the same time as trying to take care of Benjamin and Joseph, and make our home as stable and secure as possible. They too were going through the trauma of divorce, and I needed to be there for them. My friends were such strength to me and even helped with meals and looking after the boys. It all felt like such a big mess, and they walked beside me helping to try to clear it up.

I put on about eighteen pounds in weight in the months after George left, and began to suffer with plantar fasciitis.[49] I had excruciating pain in both my feet, and cried daily as I drove long distances in the car to work, and tried to walk. This continued for a year and four months and then suddenly disappeared.

---

[48] Margaret Fishback Powers (1900-85), https://www.spirare.name/footprints-sand-margaret-fishback-powers/ (accessed 19.5.20). The original authorship of this poem is disputed.

[49] Inflammation of the plantar fascia, which connect heel bone to toes.

I realised I needed to find ways to take care of myself. I visited a clinic in Anápolis, where they care for missionaries and pastors in times of crisis. It was an amazing two weeks of counselling and inner healing, and I returned to São Paulo refreshed and able to continue.

I also began Pilates lessons, which I continue to this day. My scoliosis[50] has troubled me ever since my dancing days, and I suffered with continual lower back pain. Pilates helps so much, and I am even beginning to regain my flexibility. It is a time, twice a week, just for me, and has made a huge difference to my body and stress levels.

Another new hobby was gardening.

'Cally, your garden walls are filthy,' my Brazilian friend Fran said to me shortly after George left.

'Are they?' I replied, and looked out of the lounge window at the walls. I realised that Fran was right. They were indeed a dirty shade of brown instead of white. I rent a house which is very close to a reservoir, and the humidity in the air causes a brownish-green type of fungus to grow on the walls. I had been so consumed with all the problems I hadn't even noticed they were so dirty.

'You could hire a powerwash machine, and I can get my son to paint them for you. We'll do it while you're in England during the summer,' she offered.

'Oh, Fran,' I sighed. 'I know you mean well, but it really is too much effort to sort it all out. I'll have to hire the machine and buy the paint. I haven't got enough money, and I don't know if I can be bothered.' Anything extra just seemed to be too much effort.

'Please Cally,' she insisted. 'It'll look so much better, and we'll have it all ready for your return.'

---

[50] Curvature of the spine.

So, Fran and her son washed and painted the walls, and they certainly looked much better. The house has a large garden, with lots of trees and plants, including two huge avocado trees. However, there were no flowers.

'Cally, why don't you plant some flowers?' Fran asked.

'There isn't any point,' I replied. 'I can't even look after cacti. How am I going to keep flowers alive?'

'I'll help you.'

'But I don't have any money to buy flowers, Fran.'

'Hmm,' Fran answered. 'Well, as soon as you have some, you need to plant some flowers.'

A couple of weeks later my friend from Horsham in West Sussex wrote me an email message. She had celebrated a 'big' birthday not long before, and instead of receiving presents asked for gifts of money. She wanted to bless me and the charity that helped her husband before he died. She divided the money in half, and sent £310 to me. Her words were: 'I would like you to do something special with it, just for you.'

What a wonderful surprise and answer to prayer. I decided to buy some pots and flowers, and an umbrella for the garden table. I also bought a little bench and a bird table. I felt such joy in making something beautiful, and decided to call it 'O jardim da PazAm', or: 'The Garden of Peace and Friendship'. (It's a play on words joining the beginning of the two words 'Paz' (Peace) and 'Amizade' (Friendship).)

I wanted this little corner of my garden to be a place of peace, where I could pray and listen to God. Also, I wanted it to be a place where my friends could come and have coffee and a chat, a space to find peace in their busy lives. I watered the garden every day, sometimes with my tears, and it's still a great source of joy to me. I discovered recently that one of the best treatments for depression is gardening!

God spoke in a miraculous way to both George and me before we met. A friend told George that God would give him a beautiful flower from His garden, and this person would be his wife. God told me that he would give me a husband, and that I was a beautiful flower in His garden. This was something someone said to me while I was studying at King's Bible College. A few weeks after George and I started going out he asked me, 'Cally, are you a beautiful flower in God's garden?'

'Yes,' I replied. That wouldn't have been my normal response as my self-esteem was still so low, but I knew what God had said to me. That was one confirmation for George that I was the right one.

Now, a few months after our separation I was sitting in my garden, and crying out to God.

'What about the beautiful flower in your garden?' I asked. There was a moment of silence, and I sensed God reply, 'You are still a beautiful flower in My garden, nothing alters that.' I cried some more, and realised that my marriage break-up doesn't define me, and that I am beautiful and precious in God's sight.

Something, however, troubled me deeply. I felt a sadness deep inside me that just wouldn't go away, and I couldn't really understand why I felt like this. In many ways my life was so much better than before. In a strange way it was a huge relief to be free, and not under a level of constant stress.

So, why did I feel this deep sadness that just wouldn't go away? I prayed and asked God to show me. I was sitting on the sofa in my living room, praying and listening to God. I asked Him to help me understand the sadness I was feeling, and I began to weep for several minutes.

Suddenly I realised I was crying because my dreams were over. My dream to be married and live with George until parted by death.

My dream of developing the project and helping people together. My dream of growing old beside my loved one, and watching our sons grow into men. My dream of looking after our grandchildren together, and of travelling and enjoying new experiences.

The dream was over, and I realised that this was the deep sadness I was feeling. As the days went by I felt the sadness slowly lifting, and I began to feel better within myself. I felt as though once I had identified it, then it didn't overwhelm me anymore. I still feel sad, even today, but not in the same way as before. I still have moments when a wave of grief suddenly overcomes me, but I know and accept this as part of the process of moving on.

I am also very grateful for the support I have received from George's family. They treat me as though I am a true member of their family, like a daughter, sister, aunty and cousin. I feel accepted and loved by them in a very special way, and they have made a huge effort to include me and my sons in family gatherings and special occasions. If I had lost them as well as George it would have been so much more painful and difficult to bear.

I arrived back in São Paulo at the end of our trip to England in July of 2017. George and I had separated a few months before, and I was still trying to come to terms with all that had happened. Friends in the UK suggested that I shut down everything here in São Paulo and returned to England. I know they meant well, and in many ways I wanted to run away, but I really wanted to stay. This is my home, and the nation God has called me to.

Financially things were extremely tight and I was struggling to pay the bills. However, God was so faithful and within a few weeks everything was paid off. I also started making cupcakes and selling them to friends. It wasn't easy baking and icing hundreds of cupcakes in my little kitchen, and I did it with tears streaming down my face. However, God honoured me and provided for everything I needed.

I applied for a divorce and had to pay for it myself, as George was unemployed. I cried out to God and said, *Lord, I need to pay for the divorce, and I don't have the money. I need 1,000 reais by Friday, Lord, for the first payment. I absolutely refuse to ask my supporters for this money. I didn't want this divorce, and I'm not asking them to help me. Lord, please could You ask someone!*

I went downstairs and turned on my laptop. There was a message from a friend here in São Paulo.

Cally, I'm so sorry I forgot to ask you last time I saw you. Do you need any help financially? Please let me know.

My mouth fell open as I read her words. I had literally just prayed, and God had already answered.

'Wow, thank you, dear friend,' I replied. 'I just prayed for God to help me, and then I read your message. I'm crying as I write this. Thank you for being so sensitive to the nudge of the Holy Spirit.'

I didn't tell her how much I needed, and later that day she brought round an envelope full of money. There was 1,000 reais inside, exactly what I needed to pay for the first instalment of the divorce.

It's still really difficult for me to say, 'I'm a *missionary*,' and then say, 'I'm *divorced.*' It feels like the two words don't go together. There's a lot of prejudice around divorce, especially within the Church, and often a lack of understanding and compassion. I never imagined George and I would divorce. I said my vows and I meant them.

Divorce is like a bereavement, and it takes a long time to mourn and move on. I realised I needed to give myself time to grieve. I also made some important life discoveries.

I learned that good friends are so important, especially those who don't gossip! I have also come to realise that life is about moments. There isn't such a thing as a 'good' year, or a 'bad' year. Maybe some years are more difficult than others, and I certainly know that is true. Recently I received the sad news that my mother had died. It was 3 January 2020, and the first week of the New Year. I felt this didn't mean the year was going to be bad; it just had a difficult start. On reflection, 2020 has turned out to be one of the most challenging years in world history with the arrival of the pandemic Covid-19! No one would have imagined 2020 would turn out this way. I have certainly learned a few lessons, like the importance of taking life at a slower pace, and finding creative ways to be in contact online with loved ones and friends.

I've also learned that sometimes you have to accept that the path your life has taken isn't the one you would have chosen. At first it doesn't seem possible, but it is possible to find happiness along that different path and enjoy the journey.

I'm learning to be kind to myself, and that doesn't mean eating lots of chocolate or foods that I think will bring me comfort. Taking care of myself means eating healthily and exercising, getting enough sleep and making time to rest.

I'm learning to say 'no' and not feel forced to make choices that please others, and cause me to feel even more tired. Self-care is also about not pressuring myself to be someone I'm not. It's about deciding to leave the dirty dishes and go for a walk, or have quality time with my sons. If someone arrives and sees my dirty dishes, I'm not a failure. I'm the opposite because I've made a conscious choice to look after myself and my family.

I've always struggled with being alone, and much preferred the company of others than my own. I'm now learning to enjoy my solitude, and sometimes surprise myself by choosing to be alone. I saw a message on the internet recently:

> You come home,
> make some tea, sit down
> in your chair, and
> all around there's silence.
> Everyone decides for
> themselves whether
> that's loneliness or freedom.[51]

That really helped me to accept my situation. I can fight it, hate it, or accept it. It isn't what I had hoped for. It certainly isn't what I dreamed of. However, I have so much to be thankful for, and life goes on, despite the setbacks. People say I must be really strong to have endured all the pain I have been through. I don't know if I'm strong, but I know I'm dependent. Dependent on God to carry me through the storm. I am unashamedly dependent on Him, and it's God who makes me strong.

I have also been able to forgive George, which is an essential part of moving on. I teach and preach about forgiveness, and am aware that it's a process. It isn't a feeling, it's a decision, and I know that my emotional well-being depends on it.

I like to describe forgiveness as similar to an onion. The first step in forgiving someone feels almost impossible sometimes, like the outer layer of the onion which is so difficult to remove. Then the following layers of the onion need to be removed one by one, and as you cut into the onion it makes you cry. Forgiveness is a painful process and needs to be faced one day at a time. Although I am still

---

[51] Author unknown, https://gomcgill.com/you-come-home-make-some-tea-sit-down-in-your-chair-and-all-around-theres/ (accessed 15.2.20).

sad and disappointed I know I have forgiven George, and am able to pray for him and ask God to bless him.

When George left I moved into the spare bedroom, and decorated it to my taste, which is very feminine and pretty. On my wall there is a saying, and I look at it every day,

> Life isn't about waiting for the storm to pass,
> It's about learning to dance in the rain.[52]

The storms in my life are constant. Sometimes it feels like the battle never ends. However, I am smiling again, laughing again, and learning to dance in the rain.

---

[52] Vivian Greene, motivational speaker, PassItOn.com.

Chapter Thirty: The Women's Prison

People will forget what you said. People will forget what you did.
But people will never forget how you made them feel.
Maya Angelou[53]

In 2017 I was invited to speak at a conference on 'The Church and The Prison System' in Belo Horizonte. I spoke about our work in the youth prisons in São Paulo, and how we use psychodrama to help the boys find different ways of thinking and behaving. I met a man there from São Paulo.

'Cally, now I understand why I had to come to this conference. I'm one of the chaplains of a group of churches in São Paulo called *A Igreja Batista do Povo.*[54] I lead a group in my church that visits the women's prisons every week. Would you come and talk to this group about what you do in the youth prisons?'

'Of course,' I replied, 'but would it be possible to do psychodrama there?'

---

[53] Arthur Austen Douglas, *928 Maya Angelou Quotes* (Scotts Valley, CA: CreateSpace Independent Publishing Platform, 2016).
[54] The People's Baptist Church.

'It would be amazing,' he said. 'We lead church meetings for the women with a time of worship, a sermon and prayers. However, we are one of many churches that visit the women, and it feels so superficial.

'There was a riot in one of the women's prisons a few years ago,' he continued, 'and several "religious visitors" were held hostage. After that the rules were tightened for all churches visiting prisons. We have to hold our meetings on one side of the prison bars while the women stand on the other side.

'I'm sure you can imagine how difficult it is to encourage the women to come closer and listen to what's being shared. My group members and I long for a way to reach the women more effectively, and also accompany them after their release. If we could start the psychodrama it would make such a difference.'

A few weeks later I visited his group and shared about our work. Everyone was so enthusiastic, and I agreed to lead a group at one of the women's semi-open prisons. However, there was just one problem. It was situated on the other side of São Paulo, a very long way from where I live. I would have to wake up at 5:20 a.m. and drive along three motorways to arrive there by 9 a.m. The traffic in São Paulo is chaotic in the rush hour, and if I left later than 6:30 a.m. then I wouldn't arrive in time. However, I agreed to do a pilot project of ten weeks, and then hand over the group to someone else.

It took about six months for the project to be approved, and in August 2018 Laisa and I began the first group. We were given the library as our working space, a small room that is very hot during the summer months. However, there are no bars between us and the women, and we can talk openly, join hands as a group and give as many hugs as we wish. This room also has windows with no bars and overlooks the street.

During the first session a young woman began to cry when it was her turn to speak.

'I live in this neighbourhood,' she said, looking in the direction of the window. 'This is the first time I've seen the outside world for six years.'

We all cried with her, and I held her hand as we stood looking out of the window.

'You know, the women don't want to do anything here,' the Director of Health and Social Inclusion told me. 'They only want to find work, as then they're allowed out of the prison during the day, which is obviously better than staying here. Also, they get paid for working and their sentence is reduced. When there isn't any work available they just want to stay in their cells, and not participate in any lessons or courses. However, your course has a waiting list. All the women want to take part!'

What a blessing. We realised that this was an opportunity to help these women reflect on their past, and make decisions that would help them to not reoffend in the future. At the beginning of the project, however, just before our first session a couple of friends were quite discouraging.

'You won't be able to work with the women,' one told me. 'They have big barriers up that prevent anyone getting close.'

'They won't want to open up with you,' another said, 'and it will be really difficult to lead the sessions.'

I was aware that it wouldn't be easy, but that kind of discouragement doesn't put me off. In fact, it makes me more determined than ever. I prayed that the women would open up and that God would use us as instruments in His hands for healing and restoration.

Ten women had been chosen to take part in the first group, and one by one they arrived. Each was dressed in a white T-shirt, brown cotton trousers, and on their feet they wore flip-flops. I was struck by the fact it was the same uniform as in the men's prison. Some had their fingernails and toenails painted and were wearing bright red lipstick. Others were less well-presented, some with teeth missing, and their hair matted and frizzy.

All were wearing an ankle band fitted with an alarm that tracked their every move. This was specifically to monitor those who were allowed to go out of the prison during the day to work. I didn't understand why they had to wear them even if they weren't leaving the premises. We greeted each one with a big hug, and sat in a circle.

'My name's Cally. I'm a missionary from England, and I'm a teacher and psychodrama therapist. I've lived in São Paulo for twenty years, I have two sons, and live in the south zone of the city, far away from here.'

The women raised their eyebrows in surprise that I lived so far away.

'And I'm Laisa. I'm a psychologist and psychodrama therapist too. I also have two sons, and live in the north zone of São Paulo.'

'So, I'd like to explain about our project,' I continued. 'Does anyone know what we're going to do here?'

They all shook their heads.

'This project began in the youth prisons. We really wanted to help the boys to not reoffend after they leave the prison. We're currently working with our fifteenth group in one youth prison, and our fifth group in another. We're seeing amazing results with the boys, and most of them have not reoffended.'

The women were listening carefully and seemed keen to know more.

'Do any of you know about the *Igreja Batista do Povo* who come here to lead the church meetings?' I asked. One or two of the women nodded, and I continued, 'So, we were asked by the church to lead a project for you. These sessions will happen once a week for about three months, and we'll also help you and your family after your release. We know how difficult it is to get work and adjust back into society after being in prison for so many years, and we really want to help you.

'These sessions are a place where you can feel free to express yourselves in a place of trust and confidentiality. No one's going to share what you say, and we don't write any reports for the judge or the judicial system. Every session will begin with an opportunity to share how you're feeling. We'll pass an object around the circle and you can share whatever you like. You also don't have to share if you don't want to.

'This idea comes from the ancient customs of indigenous tribes and is a theory called "Peacemaking Circles",'[55] Laisa said. 'It's about creating a "safe place" where you can share your feelings and thoughts without being judged. When you're holding the object you have the right to speak, and everyone else has the right to listen. There isn't any right or wrong, as your opinion is valid, whatever it is.'

I remembered my friends' 'advice' that the women wouldn't open up, and held my breath, wondering what would happen next.

Would they just look at me, and Laisa, and keep quiet? Would there be an awkward silence for the next few minutes?

'So, I'll start.' I said. 'Um… I'm really happy to be here. We've waited six months to start this project, and I'm extremely excited to meet you all.'

I passed the object (a small toy monkey) to the woman on my right, my heart racing with anticipation.

'How are you feeling?' I asked gently. 'What are your thoughts as you take part in this group for the first time today?'

---

[55] See Kay Pranis, Barry Stuart, Mark Wedge, *Peacemaking Circles* (St Paul, MN: Living Justice Press, 2003).

The woman smiled and said enthusiastically, 'I'm so happy to be in this group. I can't stand it in this prison any longer. I feel like I'm going to go mad. Thank you so much for coming here to help us.'

All the women expressed similar feelings, and everyone said at least a few words.

That wasn't a bad start, I thought to myself. *I wonder what insights these sessions will bring, and if the psychodrama will be helpful to these women?*

I certainly shouldn't have worried about the women not wanting to participate. The sessions were an opportunity for them to say what they so desperately needed to say. In their cells they were often frustrated and unable to be sincere about how they really felt. At the beginning of our sessions they arrived so stressed, and often full of anger. By the end of the session they felt relieved and grateful to have had the opportunity to express themselves.

'Cally, you'll never guess what happened,' one of the women exclaimed, as she sat down in the circle at the beginning of one of the sessions. 'This week there was a moment in our cell when everyone was shouting at each other and nobody was listening. It was chaos. I picked up an empty pot, and held it up in the air. Everyone turned to look at me, and I said, "Listen. Everyone sit down, and we're going to pass this pot around the cell. Everyone will have a chance to speak. However, you can only speak when you're holding the pot. The rest of the time you listen. OK?"

'Cally, it was amazing. Everyone was able to share their feelings, and nobody shouted or got angry anymore.'

We were so happy to hear this.

Our goal, as we continue these sessions, is that they will spread over into the daily life of the prison and have a powerful effect in the lives of the women. We also recognise the need to work with the guards, general staff and directors. They need to be helped and cared for too. Their jobs are highly stressful, and many prison officers commit suicide as a result. In September 2019[56] we were invited to lead a session with the staff on the theme of 'Suicide'. Sixteen members of staff took part, and all said it was extremely helpful, not only to recognise their own needs, but also to be aware of others.

The following week I arrived at the prison and one of the directors greeted me with these words: 'The members of staff have asked for more sessions, Cally! Can we try to do one a month?'

'Yes, of course,' I replied. 'That is wonderful news. I know the sessions will make a big difference for the staff and the whole prison.'

Even more wonderful news was waiting for me as I walked into the library to take the session with the women prisoners.

'Cally, everything has changed since that session you did with the staff,' one of the women said. 'They treat us differently now. They praise us when we do something right, and we were even given apples as a treat!'

I think that was one of the highlights of my year. To hear that the sessions with the staff were not only helping them personally, but also helping the women was the best news I could hear. At the time of writing, we are hoping to lead monthly psychodrama sessions for the prison staff, and are excited to be able to help them in this way.

I've learned so many things through my work with the women. I know in my own experience that I need to talk to my friends about the situations I face. Rarely do I find a solution to my problems or am able to change the situation just by talking. However, just being able to express myself and talk about it makes me feel so much better.

---

[56] As part of the Setembro Amarelo campaign (Yellow Ribbon suicide prevention programme) which happens every September in Brazil, see https://www.setembroamarelo.com (accessed 19.5.20).

It's the same for the women in our groups in the prison, and the members of staff.

Their stories are so tragic. One of the women has been in prison for nine years for organising the murder of the man who raped her two-year-old daughter. Many are 'victims' of their boyfriend's or husband's actions. The men are drug traffickers, and when they get caught, the girlfriend or wife goes to prison for being their 'accomplice'. One girl was in the passenger seat when the police stopped her husband and checked the car. They found a suitcase full of cocaine, and she was put in prison for seven years as well.

They are fearful about what will happen when they are released. They know that if they continue living with the same man then they run the risk of being imprisoned again. However, they fear for their lives if they decide to leave the relationship, and as a result feel forced to continue without knowing how to escape.

One woman drank bleach, took pills and put a rope around her neck. She couldn't endure the rejection from her daughters, and so many years of suffering in prison. She was in prison for their whole childhood and adolescence and couldn't forgive herself. She was found hanging in her cell, purple and not breathing. She was revived and survived, but continues to suffer deep depression.

I knew something was terribly wrong the moment she walked into the room. Her walk was slow, and her head hung low. She sat in a heap on the chair, her shoulders tense and hunched over. When it was her moment to speak, she shared her story, and we all cried with her. When she finished I said, 'Does anyone identify with some of her feelings? If you do, then please leave your seat and go and place your hand on her shoulder.'

One by one the women stood up and walked over to her side and placed their hands on her shoulders and back. Laisa and I joined them, and I said, 'We want you to know we're with you in this. We'll never know or understand exactly how you feel, but we're with you, OK?'

She looked up at me through her tears, and for the first time I saw her smile. We all hugged her tightly, and she breathed a long sigh of relief. From then on she took part in every session, and I was delighted to watch her smile and laugh during the games and activities.

I have just finished leading our third group at the women's prison, and intend to continue. I now work there with Daniela, who is a psychodrama therapist, and Marcela, who is a dance teacher. I enjoy working there so much I can't stop just because of the long distances I have to travel. It is a sacrifice I happily make, as I can honestly say I feel like I was born to do what I do. It isn't a job. It's a privilege.

Chapter Thirty-one: Evangelist's Heaven

Continue to be who and how you are, to astonish a mean world
with your acts of kindness.
Maya Angelou[57]

Brazil is like a heaven for evangelists. People are so open to hear about Jesus it's possible to talk about Him, or show His love everywhere you go. A couple of years ago I was chatting to a friend, a young woman who is very poor, but loves the Lord.

'Cally, this week I was on my way home, and a young lad walked past me,' she said. 'He stopped, turned around, and said to me "*Jesus te ama!*"' ('Jesus loves you!') She went on, 'Then he continued walking. I was *so* blessed to hear him say that. Things are so difficult in my life, and I really needed to know that Jesus loves me. Isn't that amazing?'

Her words struck deep into my soul.

If a young lad can do that and make such an impact in someone's life, then surely I can do that too, I thought to myself. *It's just three short words, and yet it's such a powerful thing to say. Lord, from now on I'm going to tell people You love them wherever I go, I promise.*

---

[57] Arthur Austen Douglas, *928 Maya Angelou Quotes*.

One of my favourite places to tell people Jesus loves them is when I pass through the tollgates on motorways. In São Paulo many people avoid paying the toll fee in cash by signing up to a system called 'Sem Parar' ('Without Stopping'). The toll fees are calculated in a monthly payment, deducted from a person's bank account at the end of the month. A small barcode is stuck onto the inside of the car windscreen, and every time a driver passes through the tollgates, or car park entrances, the sensor picks up the details and sends it to their account. This saves time for motorists, as they don't have to sit in long queues at the tollgates, or find the payment machines in the car parks.

I have installed *Sem Parar* in my car for when I need it. However, I like to make a point of stopping at the tollgates to tell the person working there that Jesus loves them. I wait in the queue, roll down my window, hand them the money, and say, 'Hello! I actually have *Sem Parar*, but I stopped to tell you that Jesus loves you!' They are always surprised, and so grateful to hear this. I think they're amazed that someone who has *Sem Parar*, and could easily have sped through the automatic barrier, has decided to stop and wait in the queue. Somehow, that makes it all the more powerful. They always thank me profusely, and tell me Jesus loves me too.

A few weeks ago I was returning from church. I had just preached and was tired and hungry. I was going to stop at the tollgate, but the queues were long and I decided to go through the automatic barrier instead. I literally felt my car pulling to the left and taking me into the lane where I would need to stop and pay. I decided to obey, and slowed down to take my place in the queue. When I eventually arrived at the tollgate I said the same thing as always, 'Hello! I actually have *Sem Parar* but I wanted to stop to tell you that Jesus loves you!'

The woman in the tollbooth gasped, and said, 'Thank you so much for telling me that. I really needed to hear that today. My husband died in a drowning accident six years ago, and today I heard that two very special friends died. I am so sad, and I really needed to know that Jesus loves me. Thank you so much.'

Wow, I am so glad I stopped that day. We never know what's going on in people's lives. Sometimes we need to slow down enough to tell someone Jesus loves them.

I also like to pay for the car behind me at the tollgate whenever possible. I stop and tell the person in the tollbooth that Jesus loves them. Then I say, 'I'd like to pay for the car behind me too, please. I don't know the person/people but I really want them to know that Jesus loves them too. Please tell them I paid for them as a small gift, and tell them Jesus loves them.'

It's such fun to look in my rear-view mirror as I drive off. The driver behind stops, and when they put out their arm to pay I can see the person at the tollbooth telling them their car is paid for, and that Jesus loves them! It's such easy evangelism, and such a wonderful way of showing God's love.

I was so sad when I visited the UK recently. I always used to tell the person in the tollbooth at the Dartford tunnel that Jesus loved them, and would pay for the car behind. I discovered, however, that now the payment can only be made online, and I was disappointed my motorway evangelism could continue no more.

I feel very blessed to have been called to this nation where people are so open to know about Jesus. Many years ago, George and I went to Guarulhos airport to drop off a visitor. On the way out, George gave the young woman at the pay station a New Testament. George's dad was a Gideon and our car was always full of New Testaments ready to give people that we met.[58] George drove away and in his rear-view mirror saw a young man racing after the car.

'Wait, wait!' the young man shouted. Out of breath he arrived at the car, and George rolled down the window.

'I'm so sorry,' the young man puffed. 'I saw you giving the New Testament to my colleague. Please could I have one too? I don't have a Bible, and I really want one.'

'Of course,' George replied, handing him a New Testament. 'God bless you.'

We drove away overwhelmed by this young man's hunger and thirst for the Word of God, grateful for our own Bibles, and more determined than ever to read them. I also felt overwhelmed once again at the privilege of being called to this nation.

I am able to live and work here in Brazil because of the financial support I receive from friends and churches in the UK, Brazil, and around the world. I have learned the importance of saying 'thank you', communicating frequently about my work, and asking for prayer.

In 2006, one of my financial supporters asked if I could email a weekly prayer letter to my friends in the UK. She felt I needed constant prayer and wanted to know how to pray more effectively. It seemed an impossible task at the time but I have managed it every week or fortnight for the last fourteen years!

I am absolutely certain that those prayers and intercessions have made a huge difference to my life and work here. Every Sunday afternoon I sit down and write my prayer letter, including items for prayer and reasons for praise. It is a part of my routine that has become such a blessing that it never feels like a burden or chore.

I'm always delighted to meet friends when I visit the UK, who

---

[58] Gideons International is an evangelical Christian organisation that distributes Bibles free of charge.

greet me, saying, 'Cally, it's so good to see you. I pray for you every Monday morning when I open your prayer letter.' God is so faithful, and has given me so many good friends who are part of my journey, praying for me and supporting me faithfully, despite the thousands of miles between us.

Chapter Thirty-two: The Last Chapter

There is no real ending. It's just the place where you stop the story.
Frank Herbert[59]

This is the last chapter of this book, but it's certainly not the end of my story. I'm fifty-five years old now, and am sure I will have many more experiences and stories to tell. I thought that writing a book would be a wearisome and difficult experience, but it has been a wonderful journey, and I have so enjoyed telling you my story. There are many parts I have left out and people I haven't mentioned. Maybe my next book will tell their stories too.

The last few years have been a huge challenge, and much like a rollercoaster ride in many ways. George and I were divorced in 2017 and my father died in 2019. Six weeks later I lost my beloved father-in-law, George's dad, who was like a real father to me in so many ways.

This year my mother passed away, and I've had the chance to reflect again on the challenges of being a missionary. When God called me to Brazil I knew that I wouldn't be present for my parents' passing.

---

[59] https://www.goodreads.com/quotes/34036-there-is-no-real-ending-it-s-just-the-place-where (accessed 15.2.20).

Every time I visited I knew that I might be saying goodbye for the last time. That wasn't easy for any of us, but it's part of the call, and I accept it as God's will for my life.

I also felt that my move to Brazil would be permanent. People asked me, 'Cally, are you going for a year, or two years?'

'No,' I always replied. 'I'm going forever.'

A few days before I left the UK in 1999 a good friend from Milton Keynes, Colin Flack, confirmed what I was feeling.

'Cally, I've been praying for you,' he said, 'and I feel that God is calling you to be like Ruth from the Bible. You will leave your nation and join a new nation. You will leave your people and join a new people.' That was twenty-one years ago and the feeling is stronger now than ever before.

My role at the moment, as president and coordinator of The Eagle Project, is to develop the organisation and make it self-sustainable. My goal is to leave it in the hands of others who have a similar vision and passion for the restoration of those who long to be restored.

I have often reflected on the fact that God confirmed my call to Brazil through a skip, or in other words, a place where people throw their rubbish. Today my work is with those whom society has thrown away. They are robbers, kidnappers, murderers and drug traffickers. They are considered rubbish, with no hope for transformation.

However, I know there is hope. I have opportunities daily to delve deep down into that skip and find a treasure that someone has thrown away. A person who I can then take by the hand, with great care and kindness, and help restore to wholeness. They don't deserve it. They just deserve punishment. But as I once heard, 'Love isn't for those who deserve it, it's for those who need it.'[60]

---

[60] Source unknown.

No one is born a thief, a murderer, or a drug trafficker. Inside all of us is our 'baggage' that we carry on our life journey; our traumas, anger, fear and pain. We have the choice to be broken, or to seek wholeness. We have the choice to break, or to bring healing. I have the immense privilege of being in the restoration business, finding real treasure in each person I meet. I am able to help people realise how their 'baggage' and anger is destroying them and those around them. I love to reveal God's heart to those who feel unloved and unworthy and help them to be healed.

Last week a boy in the youth prison asked me, 'Why do you come here in the rain and the traffic to help us, instead of staying home in the warm and sitting on your sofa?'

'I come because each one of you is important,' I replied. 'If just one of you decides to leave crime, then it's worth all the effort. My hope and prayer is that all of you will make a decision to change. However, if just one of you makes that decision, my life will have been worth living.'

'Thank you,' he replied. 'That means a lot to us.'

My hope and prayer is that The Eagle Project will continue to grow in São Paulo, other cities of Brazil and other nations too. I believe that psychodrama is a powerful tool and I hope that many people will take this idea and use it in prisons around the world. I feel privileged to have found something that really makes a difference. When we learn to feel empathy and understand how someone else feels, that is the beginning of change. It is the beginning of forgiveness and the path to freedom.

When I was training to be a dancer, I learned the importance of perseverance. No matter the pain, the sweat, or the tears, I drove myself to be the best I could be. I persevere in my work today, not driven, but called, and determined to fulfil whatever plans God has for me. There are moments of great joy, and also of deep sadness, but I am so grateful to be doing what I feel I was born to do.

He is my all. He is my everything. And the dance continues.

God is most glorified in us when we are most satisfied in Him.

John Piper[61]

---

[61] John Piper, *Desiring God* (Colorado Springs, CO: Multnomah Books 2011).

Acknowledgements

I would like to thank my parents for always being there for me, for teaching me to have high moral standards, for supporting me in so many different ways, and encouraging me to never give up.

Malcolm Down was the first person to talk to me seriously about writing a book, and many years ago he offered to publish it. I am eternally grateful that he believed in me, and that he kept his promise.

Thank you to Sheila Jacobs for her amazing work in editing this book, and her wonderful care and patience.

I am also grateful to Ruth Leigh. This book may never have been written if I hadn't met her last summer. I timidly entrusted her to read the first chapters, and then the first draft, and her encouraging words and suggestions inspired me to press on.

I would like to thank Tom Yaccino, who was my mentor and coach during my three years in Tearfund's 'Inspired Individuals' programme. He taught me to aim higher, dream bigger and the importance of finding other people to walk alongside me on my journey. Also a huge thank you to Tim Richardson for nominating me for the programme.

I am grateful to all the Tearfund 'Inspired Individuals' team, especially Nicola Temple, Jennifer Snelling and Audrey Carmichael.

I'm so grateful to Clark Baim for inspiring me to use psychodrama in prisons. I have met Clark twice, and participated in psychodrama weekends that he has led at the Birmingham Institute for Psychodrama. He is one of the people who has most inspired me, and I am so thankful for his friendship and encouragement.

I would like to thank Andrea Calderon and Rosângela Campos for encouraging me to be a psychodrama therapist. Also to Fernanda Cezar who told me about the course on Restorative Justice.

I am eternally grateful to Beatriz Petrilli and Carolina Maroni for accepting my invitation to work with psychodrama in the youth prison. They taught me so much and were pioneers with me in this work. I write this acknowledgement with great sadness following the sudden death of Beatriz a few months ago. She was an inspiration to me, and to so many.

I am also so grateful to Laisa Teixeira Malta who has worked with me in the youth prisons since 2013. We devised and developed the psychodrama project 'Breaking the Chains' together, and I couldn't have done it without her.

Thank you to my dear friends Lynda Everson, Susanna Smoak, Helen Bizerra and Elaine Bann, for reading the first draft, and for your helpful comments and suggestions.

I am so grateful to Barrie Thompson and Frances Miles from Stewardship. They have been a constant support to me, and I am so grateful to them for reading the first draft and continuing to encourage me. Stewardship is the organisation in the UK that

channels my personal financial support, and the funding for The Eagle Project. Barrie, Frances and the team are highly professional and efficient, and make all the difference to my daily life here in São Paulo. They have become precious friends.

Anne Blair-Vincent – you are the one who introduced me to Restorative Justice and gave me the vision for the work in the youth prison. Thank you. You have played a huge part in my ministry here in Brazil.

Thank you also to Tim Nightingale for helping me to delve deeper into Restorative Justice, and for encouraging me along the way.[62]

To George, thank you for all that we did together, for all that you taught me, and for our two wonderful sons.

Thank you also to my Brazilian family who have accepted me as one of their own, and who I love so dearly.

To my friends, supporters and prayer partners – thank you. Many of you have walked beside me through my darkest times. Some of you have visited and know first-hand about my work. You are closer than family. Your financial support and prayers have given me the opportunity to serve God here in Brazil. You are part of my story and I couldn't have done this without you.

I would like to thank the Board of Directors of Associação Águia (The Eagle Project) here in São Paulo. Thank you for taking care of

---

[62] nightingaleresolutions.com (accessed 22.5.20).

me, supporting and encouraging me, and for believing it's possible to make a difference.

Thank you to my dear friend, Eloir de Paula, who has agreed to translate this book into Portuguese.

I am so grateful to Martin Brocklebank for all the chutney he has sold, and Jan Bird for all the jam.

I would also like to thank Andrew Chamberlain. I have listened to his podcasts of the Creative Writer's Toolbelt on my long journeys in São Paulo, and he has taught me so much. I am also immensely grateful that he replied to my emails, and gave me further advice and encouragement about writing this book.

Lastly, thank you to my 'spiritual' mum and dad, Tom and Jill Poulson, and all my pastors and leaders in the UK and Brazil, who have loved me, nurtured me and encouraged me on this journey.

Further Information

For further information about The Eagle Project:
www.theeagleproject.co.uk
or contact Cally at:
callyjcm@gmail.com
Instagram: cally_magalhaes / aguiaassociacao
Facebook: https://www.facebook.com/The-Eagle-
Project-170502183081714/
Portuguese: https://www.facebook.com/associacaoaguia/

The Eagle Project and Cally depend on one-off and regular donations.
If you would like information about how to support The Eagle Project
and/or Cally, please contact Stewardship at:
Enquiries: enquiries@stewardship.org.uk
Or
https://my.give.net/eagle

The Eagle Project: Ref. 20098650
Cally's support: Ref. 20035365